STOP OVERTHINKING!

9 STEPS TO ELIMINATE STRESS, ANXIETY, NEGATIVITY AND FOCUS ON PRODUCTIVITY

HARLEY HUNTER

A GIFT FOR YOU

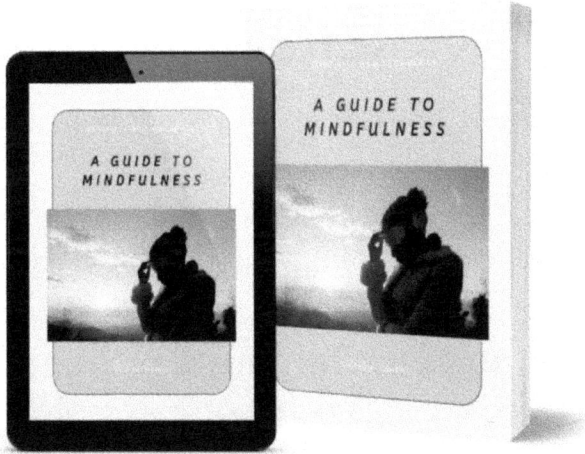

In the Guide to Mindfulness, you'll learn...

- 7 warning signs that you should start practicing mindfulness immediately
- how just a few simple habits each day can improve your focus and decision-making
- to uncover the secrets to calm your anxious, distracted mind that successful people already know

Includes mindfulness discovery exercises, workbook pages, and journal templates

Scan this Code,
or download your free copy at
harleyhunterbooks.com

AND UNLEASH THE POWER TO QUIET YOUR
MIND AND LIVE YOUR BEST LIFE!

CONTENTS

INTRODUCTION

Spend eighty percent of your time focusing on tomorrow's opportunities rather than yesterday's problems.

— BRIAN TRACY

Let's be honest; we have all been overthinkers at one point or another in our lives. Whether you have sent a risky text to a crush and are anxiously waiting for that ping that lets you know they have replied, or if you have just sat alone with your thoughts contemplating scenarios and things you could have said or done differently—these are all examples of overthinking.

Sometimes overthinking can be beneficial (or at least some people think so). Other times it only results in anxiety and disruption in productivity. When you over-think situations and scenarios, for example, it can either help you prepare for what might come, or it could just lead you down a road of anxiety, stress, and unsteadiness.

In fact, overthinking has often been linked to a lack of confidence and self-awareness. When you begin to question yourself and your actions, you cast a shadow of self-doubt on your own decision-making processes. This leads you to make mistakes you would otherwise not usually make. In addition, because of the hesitation, you may miss out on opportunities that require imme-diate attention. While you overthink things, the door of opportunity is closing. Such situations can also diminish your productivity. After all, how can you be as efficient and productive if you second-guess every little decision you make?

Additionally, when you second-guess your decision-making, you tend to become scared and anxious when faced with it. For example, when a business opportu-nity comes your way, you are likely to struggle with making even the simplest of decisions that could benefit your business. Lack of confidence and avoid-ance in decision-making can spell disaster for your chances of becoming a successful leader.

Consider the example of Tom for a minute. By all outward appearances, Tom has everything–a successful career, a loving girlfriend, and many friends. But inside, Tom is on a never-ending rollercoaster of thoughts and doubts. He constantly questions every little thing. Did he say the right thing to his boss that morning? What was his girlfriend doing for those thirty minutes she wasn't responding to his text?

Perhaps you may relate to Tom in one way or another. Maybe when you're in a crowded place, and you hear a group of people laughing, you instantly panic because you think they're making fun of you, or you feel like you're always being judged when you're around strangers (or even your friends). Maybe you can't stop yourself from constantly thinking back to past mistakes and better ways you would have approached the situation, no matter how great your life is currently. Much like Tom, these feelings are not abnormal.

Many people struggle with overthinking for most of their lives and have discovered that managing it *is* possible; there are ways to prevent our thoughts from consuming us. Throughout this book, techniques on how to manage your overthinking will be presented.

Overthinking can wreak havoc on your physical and mental health, yet many of us are too afraid to speak up about our struggles. This is because even though society has come a long way regarding mental health issues, there is still a negative stigma attached to it.

We will often rationalize our overthinking by saying we need to think about our problems in order to solve them. While this is true when deciding on something major, like whether or not to leave your job, if you continue to fixate on every negative aspect of your life, you may prevent yourself from making any decisions or actions that will improve your situation. This book will not only help you solve your problems, but hopefully, it will also help you to learn techniques that will quiet your mind and help you find inner peace. Unlock the tricks that can help you overcome your insecurities and finally stop overthinking every interaction throughout your day.

The objectives of this book are to provide you with:

- a deeper understanding of what overthinking is and why we do it.
- an insight into the impact overthinking can have on your body.
- information on what can trigger your overthinking so you know how to avoid it.
- tips on how you can minimize negative self-talk.

- advice that will help you quiet your mind and the world around you.
- discovery of the best methods of combating your overthinking.
- lessons on how to rewire your brain so that overthinking no longer takes over your life.

Being stuck in a cycle of over-analyzing every aspect of your life and second-guessing your decisions is difficult and frustrating. The hope is that this book will help you feel reassured, knowing that you're not alone and that by pressing the big red *stop* button for overthinking, you may be able to increase your focus and productivity.

1

IDENTIFYING OVERTHINKING

> *Action is a great restorer and builder of confidence. Inaction is not only the result, but the cause of fear. Perhaps the action you take will be successful; perhaps different actions or adjustments will have to follow. But any action is better than no action at all.*
>
> — NORMAN VINCENT PEALE

S ometimes, overthinking can seem like your brain's attempt at being extra cautious–like the well-known saying, *once bitten, twice shy*. Therefore, it can become easy for a person to develop this habit in an effort to prevent themselves from being *bitten* again. Many times, people have been cheated, lied to, missed business opportunities, or simply regret things they now feel should/could have handled differently.

However, overthinking can become a detrimental habit that can affect your confidence and ability to make effective decisions. You may even begin to develop anxiety as you now fear finding yourself in similar situations or decision-making processes.

Diagnosing or identifying when you are overthinking can also be tricky. Because it generally begins as a *reflex* to avoid pitfalls that you (or someone else you know) may have experienced in the past, it can be difficult to identify before it may be too late. In some instances, overthinking occurs as a result of past encounters or experiences. Overthinking can also happen because of a lack of self-awareness that can affect your confidence in your interactions with other people and your decision-making.

When a person overthinks, they either *ruminate* (go over and over in the mind) or worry continuously about something. Using this definition, many people are likely to believe they are overthinkers. After all, who does not go a single day without at least overthinking something, right? It is normal to wonder if we're making the right choices - from lamenting over small things such as picking the fastest route on your commute to work, or choosing the right restaurant for dinner, to making decisions on your children's well-being and family's safety and security.

Fader (2021) reassures that it is common to worry and overthink to a certain extent. However, it can become exhausting when you constantly think about all the things you could have done differently, second-guess every decision you make, and imagine all the worst-case scenarios in your life. Chronic overthinking can have harmful effects mentally and emotionally. For people who don't suffer from overthinking, their thoughts and worries typically disappear after a while. But when your mind wanders continuously, and you find yourself worrying about yourself, your future or past, your family or friends, or doubting every decision, you are an overthinker.

Understandably, there are times when you may continue worrying about something. But if you are an overthinker, chances are you not only struggle with eliminating your anxieties and worries, but also unwillingly allow them to interfere with your life. Worry and rumination is all an overthinking person can focus on. Even if they do not obsess about the same thing all the time, they are always concerned about something. This can make overthinking a tough habit to break.

You may even convince yourself into believing that by thinking about something for a really long time, you can develop the best solution to your problem. However, this is not always the case. In actuality, it is believed that "the longer you think about something, the less time and energy you might have to take productive action" (Morin, 2020).

Understandably, everyone tends to overthink sometimes. Perhaps you might keep thinking about all the things that could go wrong when you give a presentation next week, for example. Or maybe you have wasted countless hours trying to decide what to wear to that job interview and, as a result, did not spend time preparing your answers.

Malachi had always been cautious by nature in his decision-making and his relationships. As an adolescent, he would gaze into the nothingness and let his mind drift off, creating and replaying scenarios in his busy head. With such an imaginative mind, Kai (as he was affectionately known) would sometimes come up with scenarios for situations yet to come to fruition. In one particular daydream, he imagined all the ways he would tell his high school crush how he felt about her. Kai's thoughts encompassed all the possible answers she would give and how he would counter with a witty remark that would surely leave her amazed and impressed. Though this seemed like a good idea at the time, in preparation for all possible outcomes, little did

Kai realize that he was planting a seed that could give him much anxiety over the next decade. The internal conviction that his foreshadowing and predictive imagination helped him stay ahead of the curve became the birth child of a potentially harmful habit in his future relationship.

In the years that followed, Kai fell in love with Natasha. However, because Kai had seen most of his peers experience infidelity and commit the same, he was wary of all the ways people can be deceitful and hurtful. A few months into his relationship with Natasha (who lived in another town), his overthinking began to creep in… this time in the shape of insecurity and accompanying thoughts. Kai started to obsess about what Natasha was doing when she was not with him. He began to overthink, coming up with what he deemed were 'possible scenarios' in which Natasha might be unfaithful to him. Despite little to no evidence to prove Natasha's infidelity, these constant thoughts haunted Kai and continued to fester into toxic behaviors.

Through overthinking and trying to get ahead of the heartache and betrayal, Kai talked himself into going through his girlfriend's phone to prove himself right. The thoughts that had led him to search for evidence of infidelity had stemmed from months of overthinking scenarios and situations that had not even happened (except in his head). That, coupled with deep-seated feelings of insecurity, had driven him to show doubt and mistrust in his partner. Kai found what he thought was evidence enough to warrant interrogation. He confronted Natasha about a text message from an unsaved number asking to meet up with her. She explained the situation satisfyingly but realized she could no longer be with a person who could not trust her. She ended things with Kai, who then realized his attempts to overthink and get ahead of situations before they 'sneak up on you', had led him to become obsessed with fictional scenarios that were all just figments of his overactive imagination.

Much like Kai's story, you may have found yourself at the detriment of overthinking. Perhaps, the results are yet to be as damaging as with Kai. But overthinking can still affect your personal life, focus and work productivity.

For example, consider Jim, who always second-guesses his presentation style, thinking it is not good enough. Or Kate, who is convinced that her co-workers gossip about her at lunch because she overheard them laughing in her direction the other Monday. Because overthinking can happen as a defense (we activate it to avoid being naive and being caught off-guard), it may often go unchecked or unnoticed. It can become tough to identify when you are overthinking a situation and when you are being overly cautious.

TWO TYPES OF OVERTHINKING

Despite everyone overthinking things every once in a while, you may realize how difficult it is not to be able to quiet the constant barrage of thoughts that flood your mind and interrupt your life or productivity. Overthinking can create an inner monologue that includes two destructive thought patterns—ruminating and worrying. You may be familiar with these two:

- **Ruminating:** This is when you find yourself replaying a conversation in your head repeatedly or imagining something bad that happened before. It also involves rehashing the past with thoughts such as: *"I shouldn't have spoken up in the meeting today. Everyone looked at me like I was an idiot. I could have stuck it out at my old job. I would be happier if I had just stayed there. My parents always said I wouldn't amount to anything. And they were right."* You may sometimes beat yourself up for the decisions you have already made. Overthinking can also take a toll on your mood and confidence, and might even make it even more challenging to

make decisions in the future. You might find
yourself wasting much time thinking about
how your life could have been better if you had
only taken that other job or not started a
business, for example. Or perhaps you may get
upset with yourself for not seeing the red flags
sooner in a relationship you had with someone
—because you believe they should have been
obvious.

- **Worrying:** This involves negative—often
catastrophic—predictions about the future.
Some examples of things you may find yourself
saying or thinking are: *"I'm going to embarrass
myself tomorrow when I give that presentation. My
hands will shake, my face will turn red, and
everyone will see that I'm incompetent. I'll never get
promoted. It doesn't matter what I do. It's not going
to happen. My spouse is going to find someone
better than I am. I'm going to end up divorced and
alone."*

Overthinkers don't just use words to contemplate their
lives. Sometimes, they can conjure up images. For
example, you may envision your car going off the road
or replay a distressing event that happened in your
childhood, like a movie. In any case, you may not
realize that your tendency to overthink everything will

keep you from doing something productive with your day.

HOW TO KNOW WHEN YOU ARE OVERTHINKING

The first thing to realize when identifying overthinking is that it can often feel like problem-solving. You may convince yourself that thinking hard about a situation and trying to find all possible outcomes is the key to solving a problem. However, the two are definitely distinct.

Problem-solving is when you ask questions with the intent of finding an answer and enacting a solution. For example, you may ask yourself: *"What can I do to improve my history marks this term?"* On the other hand, overthinking is when you lament about potential outcomes and pitfalls without any real intention of solving the problem. For example, *"Why did I make that joke? I think I may have offended Mike",* when, in fact, an issue or potential problem may not even actually exist.

Overthinking is also different from self-reflection (which involves looking back on your past). Overthinking can also sometimes feel like self-reflection. You may be thinking: *"What if I am thinking about the past as a way of reflecting?"*

Self-reflection can be healthy as it involves learning, growth, and gaining perspective about yourself regarding a situation at hand. Self-reflection is also purposeful. Overthinking, on the other hand, is thinking about everything you do not have control over and then focusing on how bad you feel about it. It does not help develop any insight into the situation nor help in self-reflection and growth.

"Self-reflection is an internally inquisitive process rooted in a higher purpose—whether that's to grow as a person or gain a new perspective. If you're obsessing over something you don't like about yourself that you either can't change or have no intention of improving, it's not self-reflection—it's overthinking" (McCallum, 2021).

In fact, when you overthink and focus on things you cannot control, it can debilitate you into believing you are incapable of achieving what you have tried before (and failed) and can diminish your self-confidence. Most people think that ruminating over something you may have been unable to achieve or get done in the past can help you find a solution. However, this is not always the case.

An example to help in understanding the difference between overthinking and problem-solving is: When a storm is coming, an overthinker will think, *I wish the storm wouldn't come. It's going to be awful. I hope the house doesn't get damaged. Why do these things always have to happen to me? I can't handle this".* A problem-solver would instead think, *"I will go outside and pick up everything that might blow away. I'll put sandbags against the garage door to prevent flooding. If we get a lot of rain, I'll go to the store to buy plywood so that I can board up the windows".*

However, in the moment, overthinking may still be challenging to identify.

The first step in helping you solve a problem (be it a habit or an addiction) is you need to recognize and acknowledge the problem. So, before you can put a stop to overthinking, you will have to identify when you are doing it. Here's how to know when you're overthinking. The following are some of the key signs and symptoms to look out for when identifying the habit of overthinking:

- emotional absenteeism
- sleeplessness and/or restlessness
- aggression
- excessive resentment and regret
- difficulty in understanding other people's perspectives
- feelings of loneliness

- stress
- repetitive thoughts
- finding it hard to concentrate
- performance anxiety (worrying about how you compare to others at work)
- thinking *what-if* scenarios in which you consider things that could happen in a variety of circumstances (much like what happened with Malachi in the previous story)
- catastrophizing or thinking of the worst that could happen
- worrying about having a panic attack unexpectedly
- harboring intrusive or obsessive thoughts (for example, about what people might think about you)

Overthinking can also be a result of anxiety. As you may probably already be aware, many people in the United States of America live with some form of anxiety disorder every day. Many of these people attest to overthinking as a significant symptom of anxiety disorders. When overthinking is the direct result of an anxiety disorder, the excessive thoughts cause one to experience constant stress, fear, and/or dread. Overthinking is not just thinking too much about something, but rather obsessing about something so much that it affects one's ability to function in their life.

OVERTHINKING AND OBSESSIVE THINKING

As you read through this book, you may be wondering if you are an overthinker or are obsessive about certain things. Because the two are closely linked and seem very similar, it may be difficult to distinguish the two.

However, overthinkers tend to think too much about a particular issue. For example, when you think too much about what clothes to wear to a party because you are worried about what impression you will make, or when you think about an exchange you had with a person a few days ago that may have not gone so well. You may find yourself thinking about what you could have said or done differently.

In addition, overthinking may also involve finding it difficult to follow along with and contribute to a conversation because you go over potential responses or statements in your head until the conversation has either ended or the window of opportunity for speaking has been lost. It can also either involve worrying about future tasks and goals until they feel almost impossible to accomplish.

Obsessive thinking, on the other hand, is when these thoughts and imaginations become a looping feature in your thinking. You become debilitated and unable to make any decision without thinking of the worst. The blur between overthinking and obsessive thinking can be difficult to observe as they both have similar symptoms and characteristics. However, there is another difference. Overthinking is often linked to perfectionism, while obsessive thinking is associated more directly with a condition known as obsessive-compulsive disorder (OCD) (Krstic, 2021). The key to understanding the difference between the two is to keep in mind the frequency of these behaviors, the level of distress someone feels over them, and how much it interferes with a person's life.

Like overthinking, OCD is an anxiety disorder in which people take action based on things they see as a threat. For example, this could be germs, worry about a fire, or a personal safety concern (although compulsions aren't always logically linked to an obsession). Whereas a person who overthinks would worry about whether or not they left the stove on, a person with OCD will become restless, distressed, or even go back several times to make sure the stove is off, even after they had already left the house.

When people with OCD engage in their compulsions, they may feel temporary relief from their anxiety, but this does not last as they are back constantly worrying about the same thing. The significant difference between the two is how often you have these thoughts, how intense they are, and how much they interfere with your life (Nast, 2018). It is normal for people to have *obsessions*, such as stressful thoughts that pop into their heads and feel uncontrollable. If you obsess over a problem at work but stop once it is resolved, it is unlikely that you have OCD. But if you spend at least an hour every day having obsessive thoughts about an issue and have associated rituals that make you feel better, then you may actually have OCD.

OVERTHINKING AND BIPOLAR DISORDER

When one hears the term bipolar disorder, they tend to think of the mental health information they already know. The common conception is that people with bipolar disorder tend to be either depressed or manic and alternating between the two. People with bipolar disorder experience extreme highs and lows (in the form of mood swings) that come and go. Individuals with bipolar disorder also have a difficult time handling their moods, and they may also struggle with over-thinking.

With bipolar disorder, overthinking, upsetting or distressing thoughts can occur. When an individual is experiencing an extreme low, they may overthink past mistakes or worry that their condition will keep them from being happy in the future. They might also worry about the side effects of the antidepressants they are taking to curb their disorder. When experiencing a manic episode, a person with bipolar disorder may have trouble paying attention to their thoughts. This makes it difficult to challenge their thoughts and reframe them into something positive.

Though rumination is common among everyone, it can feel impossible for a person with bipolar disorder to quiet their mind. It can also be more difficult to separate reality from fiction during a manic episode. Sometimes, bipolar episodes can last for different periods, and such negative thoughts will only worsen them. For example, if an individual only focuses on negative things, it may prolong and worsen the symptoms they are experiencing. Harmful, uncontrollable thoughts have been known to exacerbate the condition.

OVERTHINKING AND HYPOCHONDRIA

If you have ever fallen ill and did not know what was wrong with you, you have probably consulted the internet for clues. We have all done this at one point in our lives. You either do this to avoid going to the doctor and finding out that you have something you could have treated with home remedies, or you do so to *get ahead* of the illness.

While the internet may provide correct clues, some inaccurate ones will leave you worried and anxious. You may even start believing that those sniffles are something worse than they are! This condition is known as hypochondria.

Hypochondria, or illness anxiety disorder, is when a person excessively worries that they are or may become seriously ill whenever they experience certain symptoms. Also known as somatic symptom disorder, the mental condition reportedly affects up to five percent of outpatients in the United States of America (Barsky & Ahern, 2004).

Somatic symptom disorder is a chronic condition, and its severity can depend on age, tendency to worry, and how much stress a person is facing. Individuals with hypochondria may believe they have a physical illness like cancer, a brain tumor, or a terminal illness. This typically begins after they visit pages such as WebMD and self-diagnose (Newman, 2017). In most cases, they visit the doctor for confirmation, but they are informed that they are fine and that they are simply overthinking.

People who have generalized anxiety disorder, as over-thinking is medically known, are more susceptible to being hypochondriacs. Because it can be impractical and expensive to visit the doctor for every little symptom of illness you experience, most people first self-diagnose on the internet. However, most people tend to discard any worries or fears they may have after a day or two. Extreme hypochondriacs are those that meet with their doctor frequently to confirm their self-diagnosis. Despite reassurances from the doctor, no amount of discussion makes their anxiety go away. No matter how much they try to think otherwise, they are still convinced that they are sick.

OVERTHINKING AND ITS EFFECTS ON MENTAL AND PHYSICAL HEALTH

> *If a problem is fixable, if a situation is such that you can do something about it, then there is no need to worry. If it's not fixable, then there is no help in worrying. There is no benefit in worrying whatsoever.*
>
> — THE DALAI LAMA

When you constantly worry and overthink, this can often lead to issues with mental health and overall well-being. Most of us tend to pay attention to certain things now and then—a cautionary measure to keep us from making mistakes. However, some people find themselves caught up in a loop of thoughts that keep them busy and not in a good way.

Much like anyone brimming with hopes, dreams, and plans they daydream of executing, we all find ourselves constantly imagining the things we hope to achieve or buy. One may argue that such thoughts and aspirations tend to reach an *obsessive* level. However, this can be viewed as a good thing—as long as the obsession stops once the goal or dream is achieved. This is commonly known as *a healthy obsession* as it may benefit your mental well-being when you are left satisfied with your achievement. One word of caution, though: Make sure you do not allow that *healthy obsession* to become toxic, as you may run the risk of being consumed by it.

Let's look at Todd, a 32-year-old salesman whose healthy obsession was to make salesman of the year at his job. Todd was a hard worker in his own right, but he struggled a bit with closing sales—largely in part due to the competition that was Mark. In an effort to overtake Mark in sales, Todd resorted to dirty means and sabotaged his co-worker. Despite Todd having a healthy obsession that kept him motivated and focused on achieving his goal, the constant, looping thoughts of wanting to beat Mark to become salesperson of the year had festered into toxicity and affected his integrity.

This vicious thought cycle can keep repeating itself and may invade healthy patterns. Overcoming overthinking may need to be practiced as soon as the effects become damaging or toxic, to break the negative cycle early as possible. The issues of overthinking extend to all aspects of an individual's life. Often people find themselves spending time lamenting self-limiting thoughts when they could be using that time to think about ways to be productive and mindful. Instead, people find themselves caught in a loop of thoughts on things they can no longer control, and situations they can no longer change. When you dwell on your mistakes, problems, and shortcomings, it increases your chances of being affected by mental health problems. You may begin to experience feelings of insecurity, self-awareness issues, feelings of inadequacy, and unworthiness.

Imagine this scenario: Suppose you are out with your friends, catching up over drinks and good food. However, despite the good company, fantastic food, and fun conversations, you find yourself preoccupied with something your boss or manager may have said to you at work during the day. This can spoil your mood and ruin the time you are meant to be enjoying with your friends! Perhaps your boss called you into her office to talk to you about your report, and now you're left wondering if it will lead to a warning. So instead of having a good time now, and focusing on ways you can improve your work later, you will just be gloomy and miserable, caught in a negative thought loop. And you would not want that, would you? Especially when you could be enjoying your time with friends.

Ruminating negatively can affect decision-making among individuals with depression. Overthinking can wreak havoc on your mental stability and peace, and as you begin to lose your peace of mind, you can develop acute anxiety. Overthinking is not categorized as a mental illness; however, it is definitely a symptom of depression and anxiety.

Overthinking is commonly associated with generalized anxiety disorder (GAD), which is characterized by the tendency to worry excessively about several things. *Someone can develop GAD due to their genes. Or it could be personality factors like the inability to tolerate uncertainty in life. And it could be life experiences. Normally, it's a combination of all three.* Despite not being recognized as an actual psychological disorder (and only a symptom of one), overthinking can increase your chances of developing a mental health condition such as depression, anxiety, post-traumatic stress (PTSD), and borderline personality disorder (BPD). Overthinking is not just something that happens in your head, despite it sometimes feeling that way. Overthinking can affect how you experience and engage with the world around you. It can prevent you from making important decisions, keep you from enjoying the present moment and drain you of the energy you need to handle daily stressors.

Also, whether you are fixating on the past or catastrophizing about the future, these thought patterns can be more destructive than constructive and can take a toll on physical health (and mental health). Ruminating about stressful events can, over time, lead to anxiety and depression. From a mental health standpoint, anxiety can affect your ability to cope with everyday stressors, and depression results in sadness, loneliness, and feelings of emptiness. Overthinking can have adverse effects not only on mental health but also on your physical (and emotional) health as well. The regular patterns of overthinking may lead to the following:

- fatigue
- headaches
- nausea
- difficulty concentrating
- anxiety
- depression

- irritability
- panic attacks
- low appetite
- irregular sleep patterns
- high blood pressure

McCallum (2021) writes: "What's more is that generalized anxiety disorder is linked to high blood pressure and poor cardiovascular health, while depression can increase your risk of heart attack and suicide."

As we all know, emotions play an integral role when it comes to keeping yourself sane. When you ruminate on certain thoughts, they can sometimes snowball into bigger, more extreme negative thoughts that can affect your self-awareness, confidence, and everyday life. When it becomes destructive to our life or really impairs our daily functioning, this is a sign that we have gone beyond healthy emotions and thoughts. If you're having trouble sleeping at night because you can't turn these thoughts off, if it's affecting your appetite, or if you're so lost in your thoughts, you're starting to isolate yourself from other people...these are all very common examples of how overthinking can impact your daily ability to function.

Ruminating on the worst possible scenarios and outcomes can be a misguided form of self-protection.

For some people, it can be kind of like a defense mechanism. So, you can sometimes automatically assume that everyone is unworthy to be trusted, and that way, you decide not to get close to anyone. You decide to protect yourself from hurt and distance yourself from an emotional connection.

Whether they are physical symptoms (such as headaches), emotional (such as low self-esteem) or mental ones (such as leading to anxiety), overthinking can become a clog in the flow of your everyday life. When you continue to overthink, you struggle with making decisions that can bring peace and make you productive in your work life. Additionally, although it may seem like a good way to solve problems, overthinking can also become an obsessive disorder that is extremely difficult to eliminate. You may also find yourself with a condition that can affect your relationships with partners, friends, and family, as you find yourself second-guessing or overthinking their actions or words.

Consider the example of Karen, who worked at the local post office. She was not very sociable in general, as she tended to keep to herself. Despite this, she shared lunches with two of her favorite colleagues, Sasha and Pam. Often she would be convinced the other workers were making fun of her and her awkwardness—which is why she hardly socialized with people. She had always found it difficult to fit in. Even in her community college, she found it hard to find a tribe. One day while she was on her lunch break, Karen entered the break room and found Sasha and Pam huddled with some of the other workers. They were giggling, seemingly over a juicy piece of gossip. Thinking the subject was her, and with the sting of 'betrayal' she felt (as well as all the feelings of being a pariah all these years), Karen lashed out at the group. She hurled insults in a fit of rage and tears that left her co-workers puzzled. However, what Karen had not realized was that the butt of the joke was actually their manager, who had recently been caught with his pants down. Things were no longer the same between Karen and her only friends, Sasha and Pam, who had been mortified by her actions. Karen would end up finding herself more alone and on the brink of depression.

There are many perils that come with overthinking, and it is crucial that you begin to work on this problem. Fortunately, there are ways you combat overthinking, quiet your mind and increase your focus, and productivity. The next time you find yourself second-guessing decisions, or imagining worst-case scenarios, try practicing one or more of the techniques in the following chapters to eliminate overthinking, stress and anxiety.

2

PRACTICE POSITIVE THINKING, REFRAMING, AND TALK

You gain strength, courage, and confidence by every experience in which you really stop to look fear in the face. You are able to say to yourself, 'I lived through this horror. I can take the next thing that comes along'.

— ELEANOR ROOSEVELT

One of the most common characteristics of ruminating is rehashing events of the past in a negative way. Instead of looking back on what happened (past mistakes) as a way of reflecting in order to improve, overthinkers tend to ruminate and beat themselves up over things they did. What's more, over-thinkers tend to use negative language towards themselves when they have these *flashbacks*. When a person ruminates and uses phrases such as: *"I'm so stupid, how could I let that happen?"*, or *"I'm such a loser"*, or *"I should have known I was not good enough. I'll never be good enough"*, such negative talk can increase your chances of developing depression if they are unchecked or unchallenged.

If you fail to respond positively or challenge your negative thoughts, this can sometimes keep you in a cycle of negative, repetitive thinking, which is only detrimental to your mental health. The habit of rumination can prolong or intensify anxiety and depression as well as restrict your ability to think and process emotions. Ruminating can also lead to feelings of isolation and push the people you love away.

Many times, when our minds drift off as we begin to ruminate, we may find ourselves rehashing past traumas and scenarios. However, the *darkness* of these thoughts may have defining impacts not only on the rest of your day but also may contribute to your general outlook on life. In addition, when you tend to look back on certain situations and blame yourself for them, you further lower your self-esteem. This can make overcoming similar situations or challenges all the more difficult in future.

However, when you begin to think, try to practice positive thinking and understand that you cannot change the past and only learn from it. Such acknowledgment can spell growth, content and peace of mind. As mentioned, to hone this skill, practice is essential. The brain works in the same way as a rubber band that needs to stretch a little each time until it can hold bigger objects together.

For example, if you are constantly worried about what people around you think of you, you are more likely to act in a way that is foreign to who you are. Because you are constantly ruminating over past encounters, you may begin to put on a facade in an effort to be accepted and feel worthy. Remember—when you are over-thinking (ruminating), you experience feelings of sadness, isolation and unworthiness. You may feel like you are not good enough or that no one understands you.

TECHNIQUES TO PRACTICE POSITIVE THINKING AND TALK

1. Ask Yourself How Your Thoughts Affect Your Mood: One of the first steps in practicing positive thinking when you find yourself continuously running things over in your mind is to take a step back and note how such thinking affects your mood. Does it make you feel irritated, angry, or sad? Ask yourself: *"What is the primary emotion behind my thoughts?"* You can start curbing negative thoughts by challenging your over-thinking and understanding how they make you feel; whether they contribute to your overall happiness, or whether they just leave you in a rut.

Consider an example of Josh, who is constantly over-thinking how bad his appearance is. In past encounters, his look has been ridiculed. His thoughts on what is wrong with his appearance have overshadowed him and driven him into feelings of self-doubt and lowered his self-esteem.

If you have ever experienced this, you understand how important self-esteem and confidence are in a person's social development. It would be crucial for someone who may be experiencing such thoughts to actively try and reframe them before they are consumed by the accompanying negative feelings. After asking yourself about how the negative thoughts make you feel, you need to begin challenging them by attracting the oppo-site and/or happier thoughts about yourself. For exam-ple, you can take a negative thought about how big your nose is and replace it with things you love about your-self. This is known as positive reframing.

2. Positive Reframing: One of the ways you can effec-tively combat overthinking in the sphere of positive thinking is through positive reframing. This is often confused with *toxic positivity*, which requires people to think positively—no matter how difficult a situation is. However, it is worth noting that toxic positivity is different from simple positive thinking, especially when it is used as a tool to curb overthinking. There is a significant risk that a person takes in the effort to replace negative thoughts with positive ones. Much like a person trying to get rid of an addiction or habit by adopting a new one, positive thinking may become toxic. Toxic positivity happens when an individual becomes obsessed with positive thinking.

Much like positive thinking, toxic positivity can help in silencing negative emotions and thoughts and in demeaning grief. The difference between positive thinking and toxic positivity, as research shows, is that positive thinking typically focuses on the benefits of having an optimistic outlook when a person is experiencing a problem. Toxic positivity, on the other hand, demands positivity from a person, regardless of the challenge that may be facing—potentially silencing their emotions and stopping them from seeking social support. Positive reframing allows you to acknowledge the negative aspects, but then demands you evaluate any other way to think about the situation.

For example, Abel constantly finds himself complaining: *"I just hate being a manager. On top of all these deadlines and responsibilities, it's really hard to manage so many complex personalities. It's emotionally and mentally exhausting. My job just sucks. I should've stayed at Miller Investments instead. I'm not cut out for such a big role!"* While venting may feel good for Abel, it does not solve anything. Abel is likely to continue dwelling on how much he hates his job or how bad he thinks he is at being an effective manager. Despite the very good salary and perks, Abel often finds himself ruminating on his decision to head up a bigger team in a new role. Thinking this might be detrimental to his mental health because it deters him from enjoying his work and results in him believing he is incapable. In fact, due to his lack of self-confidence, Abel may find his performance at work deteriorating significantly.

However, Abel can decide to practice positive reframing and replace these negative thoughts with: *"Things are challenging right now and I'm feeling disconnected from some things on my plate. This is a new challenge and a bigger role, but I wonder if I can change anything about this situation to improve my work and expectations about it."* Such a thought shift in patterns can give Abel the power to change his situation. He can start small, by examining what important tasks need to get done first, then either delay or delegate the rest until he is feeling less anxious.

3. Talk Positively About and to Yourself: Once you have identified how negative thoughts make you feel and have reframed them, it is important that you also learn how to talk about and to yourself. Yes, we talked about this (pun intended). This is because one of the most integral characteristics of ruminating and worrying is negative talk.

If you find yourself constantly bemoaning your past situations, worrying about your future, or continuously criticizing yourself, then you may start to develop feelings of self-loathing, low self-esteem and a general disdain of things. People who overthink hardly use positive or loving language when they worry or ruminate. They typically express anxiety about a lot of things and may exhibit undue anger over situations from the past that they have no control over.

Notable examples of negative self-talk include phrases such as: *"I don't think I'll pass that exam. I can't do anything right"*, *"I'm so stupid. I should have known better"* or *"I got a C in Science. I'll never be good at it."* It is important to note that such language is different from self-criticism, although self-criticism is normal. Sometimes a person can use self-criticism to motivate themselves into doing better. They may reflect on a past event, criticize themselves and learn from it.

Depending on how often you ruminate and talk negatively about yourself, practicing positive talk can be very difficult at the beginning. Naturally so—after all, this is probably a habit you have been practicing most of your life. For people who do not ruminate as regularly, replacing negative thoughts with positive ones can become relatively easier over time.

There are certain *catchphrases* that you can begin practicing to encourage yourself to snap out of your ruminating loop. Instead of beating yourself up over things you cannot change that happened in the past, you may want to start by acknowledging. When you acknowledge that you have no power to change the events that happened, you have begun to take your power back and control your life again. Instead of saying: *"I'm such a loser, I should have known I could not do it."* It is recommended that you challenge such thoughts by countering with phrases such as: *"I know I can do it. I just need to try again",* or *"I just was not ready, and I need to practice more",* and *"Mistakes made, but lessons learned."*

Positive self-talk cannot only help you out of the constant negativity of ruminating (which can result in a higher risk of becoming depressed). But investing in constant positive self-talk can help create and strengthen the habit of positive thinking and, subsequently, a healthier mental state. By practicing positive thoughts and self-talk, you can begin to challenge any negative thoughts that creep into your head when you find yourself ruminating. In addition, Holas et. al. (2018), suggests that by practicing positive thinking, you can also reduce your overthinking significantly.

Understandably, if you have been an overthinker for most of your life, challenging negative thoughts can be very difficult. However, it is possible to stop overthinking through positive thinking. You are encouraged to practice the following suggestions on a daily basis or whenever you find yourself drifting into darker, negative thoughts.

However, it is the language that you use that determines the difference between healthy self-criticism and toxic self-talk. The toxic effects of such negative talk can lead to feelings of helplessness, decreased motivation and have also been linked to episodes of depression. Negative self-talk has been associated with increased mental health issues and resulting tragedies (such as suicide). Negative self-talk can impair an individual from seeing and capitalizing on opportunities that could potentially change their fortunes.

Kinderman, et. al. (2013) assert that those who find themselves frequently engaging in negative self-talk tend to be more stressed. This is largely due to the fact that their reality is altered to create an experience where they don't have the ability to reach the goals they've set for themselves.

Other consequences of negative talk include limited thinking (constantly thinking you cannot do something until you actually cannot do it), not accepting something unless it is perfect (even if it is excellent or good), and insecurities.

So, the next time you find yourself overthinking and feeling like you did not do something right or you criticize yourself, it is essential to watch how you talk to yourself. Take a step back, reflect, and criticize yourself, but use positive reframing and acknowledge the mistake. This will allow for growth and keep you motivated and focused on your goals. When you look back at your past or worry about the things yet to come, try not to be so hard on yourself.

Nurturing and practicing positive thoughts are crucial in shaping your general outlook on life, family, and yourself. Always be mindful of negative thoughts that might creep up on you and try to ruin your day or view of yourself. Nip that negative thought in the bud! Replace it with a good memory instead—something from the past that makes you smile and feel all warm inside (positive reframing). Doing this will help you overcome your overthinking as you begin investing in healthier mental well-being that can lead to fulfillment, gratitude, and happiness.

Understandably, putting an end to rehashing, second-guessing, and catastrophic predictions is easier said than done. It can be tough to challenge your negative thoughts and positively reframe your thinking, especially if you have been a victim of the habit for a long time. But know that it *is* possible. With consistent practice, you can curb your negative thinking patterns.

By monitoring your thoughts and curbing ruminations through positive thinking, you can witness a transformation in your life and general outlook. It is worth noting that just like a muscle needs exercise, so does the brain, constantly requiring daily training on positive thinking and reframing. It will not be easy but remember—practice *does* make perfect. Having self-awareness is key to changing your mindset.

3

INVEST IN IMPROVING YOUR SELF-AWARENESS

> *I believe everyone should have a broad picture of how the universe operates and our place in it. It is a basic human desire. And it also puts our worries in perspective.*
>
> — STEPHEN HAWKING

One of the ways you can begin to effectively challenge your overthinking and change your mindset is by improving your self-awareness. Research has indicated that self-awareness is directly linked to feelings of self-esteem, self-confidence, and mental stability. Self-awareness is the ability to focus on yourself and how your actions, thoughts, or emotions do or don't align with your internal standards. If you're highly self-aware, you can objectively evaluate yourself, manage your emotions, align your behavior with your values, and understand correctly how others perceive you. (Duval & Wicklund, 1972)

A profile of characteristics that describe a self-aware person as a person who:

- understands their strengths and weaknesses.
- can understand and talk about their feelings.
- can acknowledge and understand other people's feelings.
- understands how their actions affect other people.
- can learn from their mistakes and develop a growth mindset.

Because self-awareness is at the foundation of all the elements that make up our personality, it is important that a person becomes self-aware in order to be able to tackle overthinking. When you are self-aware, you are fully conscious of your strengths and weaknesses. Being self-aware can help when your mind starts to ruminate or when you find yourself worrying about the future. When you know the things you are capable of, you retain the power to realize when certain things are out of your control and sphere of influence. In addition, you are aware of the strengths and weaknesses that allow you to plan for unexpected events or things you may be worried about in future.

For example, Mario, who is self-aware, tends to over-think, worrying about his future at his work. Mario has been working for his accounting firm for eleven years and recently struggled with the company's new business direction. This has left him in a vulnerable position as he constantly worries that his job could now be on the line. The board of directors has recently sent out a memo notifying employees of a potential lay-off. Though worrying about being on the chopping board, Mario realizes overthinking and worrying about the future will serve no purpose or solution to his problem. It could either worsen his performance and productivity at work, or he could focus on his strengths and make himself indispensable. Had Mario failed to be more self-aware, his overthinking would have consumed him and crippled him into retrenchment.

In addition to allowing you to realize your strengths and weaknesses, being self-aware can also help you quiet the negative thoughts and voices that can make you believe you are not worthy or incapable of being better.

One of the other examples where people overthink is when they analyze people's perceptions of them. For example, Kate is a typical overthinker who scrutinizes every interaction she has with strangers and even friends. She always wants to know what people think of her. Let's be honest—we have all been victims of this at some point in our lives. As mentioned, overthinking is quite normal and sometimes healthy. After all, how can we grow if we do not reflect or worry a bit? These feelings and thoughts tend to make us wiser, more cautious and can help us learn from previous mistakes. However, when overthinking becomes crippling, it becomes a real problem.

As in Kate's case, she can no longer do things she truly enjoys as she often finds her mind racing, questioning what people will think of her. Again, this is probably something most of us can relate to at some point in our lives. *"I don't want to dance because I'm worried about what John and the others will think of me"*, or *"My workmates probably think I'm a snob because I like to wear designer clothes"*.

Such thoughts are evident of ways our overthinking can distance us from fully embracing ourselves, who we are, and all things we like that make us who we are. Such overthinking can lead you to change your behavioral patterns to fit in and be like everyone else. However, when a person is self-aware, they understand that they are a unique individual, and people will retain different opinions and views on who they are. This affords them the power to refrain from placing any interaction they may have with someone under a microscope in an attempt to find out what they think.

PRIVATE SELF-AWARENESS AND RUMINATION

Overthinking (ruminating) can also be linked to private self-awareness. As the term suggests, this involves introspection and reflection (Sengar, 2022). This particular type of self-reflection is mainly linked with rumination. When a person reflects and *looks within his/herself*, they can either learn who they are or criticize their past faults or mistakes. These two processes are essential for character growth or development. When you look back on your past experiences where you have made regrettable choices, you typically learn from them and will act accordingly should a similar situation arise. However, most overthinkers ruminate—rehashing these regrettable situations without learning from them.

As discussed earlier, overthinking does not serve as a solution, instead; it only sends you down a dark rabbit hole of regret. Self-reflection is purposeful. When you self-reflect, you lay the foundation for how you develop feelings about yourself. For example, you may reflect on your past relationships and think that they failed because of something *you* did. Despite being a faithful, considerate person (although no one is perfect or without flaws), you may start to convince yourself you are unlovable. Such feelings about yourself could fester and affect how you approach your future relationships as well as your overall mental and emotional health.

When you practice private self-awareness, you are introspective and can reflect on your feelings, reactions, and thoughts with curiosity rather than debilitating regret. One of the key points to keep in mind when practicing reflection, and introspection is that it does not always translate into self-awareness. The general assumption is that introspection improves self-awareness because it leads to growth. After all, what better way to know our strengths and weaknesses than by reflecting on why we are the way we are, right?

However, one of the most interesting things is that people who introspect are less likely to be actually self-aware. This is because they typically fall victim to ruminating and being stuck in feelings of *why*—as in, *"Why did I choose this different career path? I would have been happier in another place"*, or *"Why did I even say anything to my friend. I should have just stayed in my place"*. Such people typically report lower job satisfaction and mental well-being. The problem with introspection is not that it is ineffective, but it could leave you stuck with negative, debilitating thoughts. The issue is that most people are actually doing it wrong.

To understand this, think about the most common introspective question: *"Why?"* We often use this question when we ruminate and try to make sense of our feelings. For example, we can ask ourselves: *"Why do I always do this to myself?"*, *"Why did I think Jacob would like me?"* or *"I'm such an idiot. Why did I not agree to that business deal?"* As it turns out, asking ourselves *"why"* when we reflect is an ineffective self-awareness question. This is because people simply do not have answers to many of the unconscious thoughts, feelings, and motives we search for.

For example, instead of thinking you got a low rating on a report because the manager has a vendetta against you or that you are incompetent, ask yourself: *"What could I have done differently to get a better rating on my report?"* Chances are that your manager actually does not hate you or that you probably did not understand the assignment!

When you pause and think of *what* you could have done differently instead of *why* something happened, you begin to witness a shift in your mindset and self-awareness. You also start to notice that it can become easier to challenge your overthinking as you are now conscious of the fact that you have no power to change the things that happened in the past. Instead of being caught in a loop in which you bemoan your past misfortunes, you can learn from these experiences by asking constructive *what* questions.

Note: There are questions that include *"what"* that are not always beneficial to growth. Questions such as, *"What did I do to deserve that?"*, which is actually a *"Why did this happen to me?"* question. Focus instead on the self-reflective questions that yield growth.

The Importance of Self-Awareness in Overcoming Overthinking

When a person practices self-awareness, they are able to view themselves from within, reflect and realign their values, monitor thoughts, control feelings, and take note of their behaviors. Being self-aware also allows a person to realize their strengths and weaknesses. When you hone the skill of being self-aware, you can help yourself overcome social anxiety disorder (SAD) (which also reflects elements of overthinking).

Marsh (2022) describes social anxiety disorder as "a mental health issue that involves a dread of social situations including performing or speaking in front of others for fear of being negatively judged". This is evidence of what overthinkers experience. Typically, as an overthinker, you may become worried when faced with a crowd or a group of people. Some of the thoughts that may occur to you are:

- *"People are going to think I'm silly or stupid if I make a mistake."*
- *"There's no way I'll be able to speak in front of that many people. I just can't!"*
- *"I'll probably puke on stage."*

The solution to deal with such feelings may be for you to start cultivating self-awareness. Through self-awareness, you can maneuver your private and public life and capitalize on opportunities as they present themselves. When you begin to understand your weaknesses and strengths, you cultivate an essential skill that can be very useful in the business world.

If you are knowledgeable in business, you may be familiar with companies performing a SWOT analysis to determine their business capabilities. A SWOT analysis helps a company realize and utilize its strengths, weaknesses, opportunities, and threats. Much like a SWOT analysis, you, too can learn how to assess your capabilities by harnessing self-awareness. When you become self-aware, you can look forward to enjoying feelings of personal control. You can monitor your thoughts and identify feelings that do not benefit you. You can also use this skill to help you decide on the right work environment that best suits you and make you productive. This can lead to higher job satisfaction.

Self-aware people are also more likely to experience healthier, happier relationships. The understanding is that when you reflect, you can see how other people view you. When you are aware of how others view you, you are often more empathetic (Betz, 2021). Typically, you become understanding of other people's perspectives and how they may feel. This means that if you are self-aware, there is a likelihood that you have a higher emotional quotient (EQ) and be able to relate to people without judging or being prejudiced. According to Lebow (2016), an emotional quotient is mainly your ability to understand other people's emotions and what motivates them. The following are some of the benefits of being self-aware as they relate to overcoming overthinking:

- **Better Decision-Making:** As mentioned earlier, lack of decision-making or constant hesitation is a key characteristic of overthinkers. When faced with a variety of choices or options, overthinkers will scrutinize every piece of information until they are left even more confused or indecisive. In business, this can typically be a good or a bad thing.

While it is recommended to analyze all angles when making a business decision, in most situations, overthinking will leave you undecided, unable to make a swift decision should there be a need for one.

- **It Improves Your Confidence:** Lack of confidence is another common characteristic of overthinkers. Because of past mistakes and future worries, people who struggle with anxiety and overthinking also often lack confidence—not just in their decision-making but also in their abilities. When you cultivate self-awareness, you become more confident and proactive in aspects of your life. You begin to understand your weaknesses and strengths and make sound decisions accordingly.

- **Multifocal Perspective:** Self-awareness also includes having an understanding of other people's views and opinions of you. When you become self-aware, you begin to see and approach issues and problems from multiple perspectives. It also means you are able to empathize with people and understand how differently they may view a similar problem. Viewing a problem from another person's vantage point may help you realize different solutions to a problem you saw in your own frame. Think of it as putting on a different pair of shades or prescription glasses.

- **You Can Free Yourself from Self-Bias:** When you become self-aware, you begin to understand and acknowledge how people view you and move away from approaching situations with bias.

- **It Helps Build Better Relationships:** When you are self-aware, you understand how your actions may affect the people around you. You will be able to watch your words or reaction when you encounter a tense or uncomfortable situation.

- **Regulate Emotions:** Being self-aware means you understand how your reaction to a particular situation may affect the people around you. Regulating your emotions is a great skill for fostering healthy relationships, even beyond your personal life. For example, in a work environment, you are able to monitor your reaction should a project be delayed because of a mistake a subordinate has made. Your response to such a situation could determine the level of respect your co-workers will retain for you.

- **Better Communication Skills:** When people become truly self-aware, they also become better communicators at work and in their private lives. You can express how you feel when you feel it and let people know what you are thinking. And because you are more empathetic when you are self-aware, you also know not to say things that might hurt others.

TECHNIQUES TO CULTIVATE SELF-AWARENESS

You may be wondering how you can take control of your thoughts, your emotions, and your life by harnessing the power of self-awareness. As outlined, being self-aware can be an effective way to change your mindset and improve your overall well-being. However, cultivating self-awareness is not going to be an easy process. In fact, experts Eurich (2018) and Betz (2021) believe that a lot of people may think that they are self-aware, meanwhile, they may actually be off the mark. You may be thinking: *"Well then, how will I achieve self-awareness and quiet my mind?"* Here are a few techniques you can follow on a daily basis:

1. Start Asking More *"What"* Questions Instead of *"Why"*: At the center of self-awareness lies the ability to look inwards and reflect on decisions and reactions. When most people reflect on their feelings, decisions, and actions, they typically ask the question *"why"*.

When trying to understand your feelings towards a past decision, you may ask yourself, *"Why did I decide to take this job when it only makes me miserable?"* or *"Why didn't I just take that business offer?"* However, Betz and Eurich note that asking "why" is not an effective way of resolving internal conflict. As humans, we do not have access to our unconscious mind—and because of this, we end up coming up with inaccurate answers to such conflicts. The recommendation then is to begin practicing asking *"what"* instead of *"why"*. For example: *"What can I do to stop feeling unhappy at my job?"* or *"What can I do to avoid losing out on another business offer next time?"* This kind of introspection will help you make better decisions in the future and avoid similar situations, signaling growth.

2. Name Your Negative Thoughts and Feelings: This will allow you to confront your feelings and emotions from a third-person perspective. Typically, when you ruminate or worry about the future, you may start blaming yourself for being weak, stupid, or incapable. But you forget that most of the events and influences that lead you to the decisions you have made are really just out of your control. However, when you put a name to a negative feeling or thought you might be having, it can give you an upper hand in confronting it. For instance, when you find yourself having negative thoughts about your job or feeling anxious about a presentation, you can personify those feelings by giving them a name—like Negative Nick. You will have the power to look in the mirror and confront Negative Nick in your head and challenge *him*. In addition, this will allow you to objectively analyze a problem or concern and probably unlock a solution.

3. Find Out What Others Think of You: Getting feedback on how people think of you does not always have to be confrontational. You might be worried that if you ask people what they think of you, they might think of you as *pretentious*. After all, it does kind of indicate self-consciousness. But remember, one of the things you may struggle with is the anxiety from trying to figure out what people think of you. This translates to being publicly self-aware—which is the other type of self-awareness (private and public). So, when you find yourself struggling with how to stop worrying about what people think about you, you may want to just bite the bullet and find out!

Approaching people and asking them, *"Hey Jim, what do you think of me?"* for example, is probably not the best way to go about it, in case you were thinking that. Try to be less blunt and more subtle. People do not always tell a person what they think of them to their face. During a conversation, you can ask them about their opinion on a matter. When they echo the same sentiments as you, you can let them know you feel the same way. In addition, putting emotions aside and acknowledging another person's valid points can signal maturity and growth. You might even learn a thing or two!

In addition, you can make this discovery indirectly through other connected parties. Asking other people, in a clever way, what a particular person thinks of you can also help you understand how your actions may have shaped this view. You may be able to find out why someone views you the way they do. Or maybe, it can even discredit whatever perceptions you thought they had about you!

4. Define Your Own Beliefs: Self-awareness is loosely referred to as knowing yourself. Because your values and beliefs develop over time, they help in defining what makes you who you are. However, because of societal expectations, you can become confused, anxious, and conflicted about how your values and beliefs measure up to other people's perceptions of you. On top of what society frames as *acceptable,* you are still expected to develop your own beliefs and values of what is meaningful. Trying to navigate people's (society's) expectations of you while trying to stay *true to yourself* can be very confusing and frustrating for a lot of people. Part of being self-aware is being able to distinguish between your and other people's beliefs and values. So, when you feel like you are under pressure to be something you are not (which can be very stressful), you may want to practice taking a step back and questioning whether you are being true to yourself in your actions. Remember to be brave enough to stand out and be unique, as defined by what you believe is right. When you do this, you will start to notice that *worrying about what people might think* will start to fade away and make you more confident in yourself and your expression.

4

DISTRACT YOURSELF

Instead of worrying about what you cannot control, shift your energy to what you can create.

— ROY T. BENNETT

Sometimes when you struggle with overthinking, stress and anxiety, you are typically faced with a range of difficult emotions, such as worry, sadness, and embarrassment. In some cases, people who suffer from anxiety and stress also experience panic attacks which are noted as the main symptom of panic disorder. When this occurs, it is often accompanied by strong emotions, including fear, uneasiness, nervousness, and apprehension.

In order to cope with these challenging emotions, many people turn to maladaptive behaviors. Star (2020) describes maladaptive ways of coping as only temporarily making the emotions go away, increasing anxiety, and can have long-term negative effects. However, one of the ways you can rid yourself of over-thinking and anxiety can be to distract your thoughts.

By practicing distraction techniques, you can be able to manage the symptoms of anxiety and overthinking. Techniques can look different for each person, depending on what you enjoy doing.

If you recall, one of the most successful viral *gadgets* that was invented to help with anxiety was the fidget spinner. As simple as it is, it is quite an effective tool to distract yourself. Other ways you can shut down those negative thoughts can be through listening to your favorite music, learning some new cooking skills by trying out a new recipe, going to your favorite workout class (yoga is pretty relaxing), taking up a new hobby (such as painting), or even going for a run!

A distraction technique is simply any activity that you engage in to redirect your mind off your current emotions (Star, 2020). Instead of putting all your energy into the upsetting emotion when you start over-thinking or feeling anxious, you can redirect your attention to something else. When you distract your-self, you can manage the strong emotions that come with anxiety and redirect your focus somewhere else.

Distraction techniques are usually often used in conjunction with other coping mechanisms. Once you have shifted your attention elsewhere and your boiling emotions have evaporated, this provides the perfect level plain to cope with emotion in a healthy manner. You will then have the opportunity to practice additional coping methods or techniques such as relaxation or other self-help techniques.

In response to the pandemic, a lot of people demonstrated distraction. At the height of the global crisis, where everyone was locked and couped up in their homes, a lot of people suffered from mental health issues (especially anxiety). Because COVID-19 was caused by a novel coronavirus that spread like a wildfire in the dry savannah it left a lot of uncertainty in the world. Global markets shook, and healthcare facilities were crippled. What's more, a lot of people lost their sources of income through retrenchments and business closures.

For those that could not afford therapy as a coping method, many turned to distraction techniques that kept their minds off the chaos. Whether this was through television series on popular streaming services (like Netflix) or by participating in viral challenges on the internet, a lot of people were able to come out on the other side.

Typically, our minds are engineered to stay busy when there is little happening. If you think back to the last time you found yourself relaxed and calm, your mind may have been *quiet*, but in actual fact, it is just idle and running on happy, calming thoughts instead. However, when people suffer from anxiety, their minds find it difficult to go to that happy, calm place—or if they do, it is extremely difficult for them to stay there. Whether addicted to a substance or a behavior, our brains have learned to associate a particular action with an outcome.

For example, when some people get anxious about something, they can start to bite their fingernails or fidget. One of the more common symptoms of anxiety is restlessness. It can really become hard to just sit still! Anyone who experiences anxiety can relate to wanting to check their news feed or go on social media when they feel anxious. In some cases, even when your mind is idle, it is almost like you become anxious because it is quiet—almost like you *should* be worried about something. When you have been suffering from anxiety for many years, you will understand what this means.

Some of the ways your body reacts to restlessness are through contractions in your stomach or chest. Because your brain is now accustomed to worrying so much, this is its way of letting you know that something is off. Your brain will *force* you to *do something!*

Finding a distraction can make you feel better and help in calming your anxiety. Looking at cute, funny cat videos on YouTube can seem like a strange choice to other people when you still have a mountain of work sitting on your desk. But to you, this is a no-brainer—survival 101. When you think about it, distraction is like the modern-day equivalent of how people avoided dangers or the unknown during ancient times. Because - let's be honest—uncertainty makes you feel anxious. And anxiety makes you want to do something.

Theoretically, that urge is there to drive you to gather the information that can help you feel at ease (Star, 2020). The problem, though, is should you find that information, it may make you even more anxious. Adversely, if you do not find any information, it also intensifies your worries. During the initial phases of the COVID pandemic, when no new information about the virus was available, people who were constantly glued to the television screen or regularly checked news websites for updates attested to not feeling any better afterward. For some, they quickly realized that finding a distraction was a pretty solid way to help calm their minds.

Sometimes in an effort to eliminate your anxiety through distraction, you may find yourself stuck in an anxiety-distraction habit loop. If this occurs, it may be best to map out the trigger-behavior-reward process that creates and perpetuates your unwanted habits. This means you need to become aware of the trigger (anxiety), the distraction behavior (such as eating, alcohol consumption, or binge-watching a television show), and the reward (when you feel better after distracting yourself from the trigger). Once you have identified the usual anxiety-distraction habit loop, you need to figure out when and how often they occur. Ask yourself if it happens in a certain context or during a particular time of day. What is the stimulus that triggers your anxiety? Then, start to explore how rewarding such habit loops actually are.

Note, your brain will choose between different behaviors, based on their respective reward levels. For example, when you feel anxious about meeting a date for the first time (trigger), your brain may choose to take a shot of alcohol (distraction), to calm your nerves (reward). The behavior or distraction, in this case, is subject to the appropriate situation or anxiety. You would not expect the same behavior if you were anxious about presenting in front of your manager or boss at work! Because all behaviors or responses to anxiety or stressful situations are not the same, there are some that are of concern. When our brain finds a distraction to cope with a stressful situation, it does so depending on the severity of the problem.

For instance, if you are dealing with a break-up from a relationship, the typical response or coping behavior that will distract you from the way you may be feeling is by drinking alcohol. This brings to attention the fact that not all distractions are good.

Brewer suggests that instead of trying to force yourself out of a *bad distraction behavior* such as stress eating (which could result in excessive weight gain and cardio-vascular diseases) or checking social media (which may only increase your feelings of anxiety), you should focus on the mental and physical results of your actions. Ask yourself: *"What do I get from doing this?"* This is not a philosophical or rhetorical question, and you are encouraged to actually answer yourself! Think about what brief relief feels like. Or how long does it last? Ask yourself if there are other behaviors that have boomerang consequences, such as getting more anxious because you have not completed a project that is due soon.

It is crucial to remember that not all distractions are bad. The problem starts when the reward you seek stops being rewarding. It may be prudent that, should your distraction become problematic, you can explore the benefits of doing less of it.

For example, if you eat a lot of sweets when you are stressed or nervous, you may want to find out how excessive sweet consumption can affect your health. Or you can explore the benefit (or lack thereof) of binging on seven versus two episodes of your favorite show. Does it make you feel better when you watch more episodes? Or does it just end up wasting your day as you become less productive? Pay attention to your coping behaviors, and how they affect you. Because your brain chooses more rewarding behaviors, you may need to identify behaviors or responses that have more rewards than your bad habits do.

This does not always mean you have to find an entirely new distraction. Sometimes it simply means stopping the behavior when the pendulum swings from being helpful to harmful. Keep in mind the phrase *"how little is enough"* when you indulge in a distraction. It is important that you apply this to all your behaviors–from eating to watching television shows, by simply checking in with your body and mind after you have indulged. Doing this will help you take stock of what behaviors are harmful and which are helpful or leave your mind quieter and more peaceful.

TECHNIQUES YOU CAN PRACTICE TO DISTRACT YOUR MIND AND RELIEVE STRESS

If you have ever had moments where you've found yourself daydreaming or just thinking about things that happened in the past, then the following tip can help you take back control of your thoughts and become more productive in your day. Perhaps you find yourself thinking about the past and think, *"Oh, I wish I had done things differently,"* or *"If only I had said how I truly felt that time".* The truth is we all find ourselves doing this at some point. And yes, while we may not want to ignore or repress our thoughts and feelings, if we allow them to take up so much energy and become debilitated, we may find ourselves feeling how we are thinking. This is where distraction comes in. The goal is to shift your focus away from harmful, negative, and depressing thoughts to those that we find engaging, positive, and that we enjoy. The key is to distract yourself the right way. The wrong way would be to indulge in harmful activities such as alcohol and drugs.

Here are some distraction techniques you can practice whenever you find yourself having negative or unwanted thoughts:

1. Cooking, Baking, or Tackling a New Recipe: This is an enjoyable technique that not only gives you (and friends or family) some tasty treats but also can help keep your mind busy and occupied with what you are doing. While cooking and/or baking may require a bit of time off the stove to simmer or bake, the initial process can help ease your mind as it requires you to concentrate on making sure your meal turns out delicious! Consider the example of Maddy, who uses baking as a pastime whenever she is stressed out. Maddy realized that by concentrating on creating the *perfect* cupcakes, she would forget her worries. In fact, baking gave her a whole new satisfaction when one of her colleagues tasted her cupcakes and wanted to buy them. By using baking as a way to eliminate her thoughts, Maddy was even able to create an extra source of income which made her happier. Her baking had paid off more than she could imagine. If you are worried about your baking or cooking skills, you can try something else from the suggested techniques below.

2. Doing Your Favorite Exercise: This is one proven way of *blowing off steam*. When you hit the gym or grab your bicycle for a ride, you allow yourself to take out whatever frustrating thoughts you may be harboring during the physical activity. When you exercise, your body releases chemicals that essentially make you feel *happier.* Take, for example, your reaction when you are stressed out or angry about something. If you take a pillow and punch it to kingdom-come, over and over all over your bed, you actually feel better afterward. You also do not need a gym membership to try this technique. As noted, you can try different physical activities to blow off steam. In fact, jogging is a great way to relieve stress (and it has added benefits too because you get in shape while you quiet your thoughts).

3. Express Yourself through Art: Whether you consider yourself to be talented or not, experimenting with pencils, paints, clay or any other form of creative media can be both distractive and cathartic. If you are unsure how to start, join a class... or, check out the countless internet videos that teach you how to draw and paint!

4. Taking Up a New Hobby: This can be anything such as journaling or collecting vintage stamps! Journaling, in particular, is a great way to channel your emotions and thoughts onto a paper. This can be a cathartic process that allows you to take note of how your thoughts and feelings affect you. As an exercise, start by writing down what thoughts have crossed your mind today. Write them down no matter how *insignificant* they may seem. Next, estimate how long it took you to get rid of these thoughts and how they made you feel. Lastly, categorize these thoughts and label them. Under negative thoughts, you can label them with a goofy name such as 'Negative Nick'. Doing this can be an effective way to take stock of how much our negative thoughts affect us and cripple our lives. Practice doing this every day before you go to bed. The more you do this, the more aware you will be when such thoughts encroach your mind. It will allow you to challenge them and positively reframe your thoughts.

5. Volunteering with a Local Organization and Engaging in Charitable Initiatives: Sometimes, when you are burdened by negative thoughts, you may feel like you are the only one going through such feelings. Anxiety and stress can fog your thinking and prevent you from realizing your humanitarian side. A good way to eliminate your thoughts is through volunteering at your local church or charity. When you realize how some people are also struggling (with mental and physiological health problems), you can find a sense of purpose that can bring meaning to your life. You can find happiness and fulfillment in helping someone who is in need. During that time, your mind will become focused on these individuals in need, and perhaps you may realize that your problems are not as big as other people's. In addition, volunteering in charitable initiatives can help you embrace gratitude for the things you have. This is an important tool in overcoming stress and anxiety.

When you practice these distraction techniques, you may start witnessing some improvement in your mood. Your mind will take a break, and you can later circle back to the issue with new and creative ways of coping with the situation. Have a look at the following example and discover how you, too, can use a distraction technique or a combination of them to overcome your negative thoughts, depression, or anxiety.

Kevon, a 34-year-old salesman from Atlanta had struggled with anxiety since his college days. He attended Howard University, a Historically Black College or University (HBCU), where he thought he would feel at home. In an effort to provide the best education for their children, Kevon's parents had moved the family out of Forest Park to a much safer, quieter neighborhood at a very young age. Despite attending an HBCU, Kevon struggled with fitting in and finding his crowd. His peers would usually call him too white to be at such a university because of his family background and status.

As a result, Kevon found himself struggling with his mental health. At parties, he would try and mingle with other students, but he always felt like there was a disconnect in the way they spoke and their shared experiences. He would try to break the ice and bring up the temperature in the room by telling a joke or two. Unfortunately, these would fall flat and just worsen his feelings and embarrassment. Kevon decided the best way to live was to just stay alone and not try to make friends.

One day, he stumbled on an article on dealing with anxiety which included tips on how to overcome your negative thoughts and feelings. After reading the article, Kevon decided to try journaling and trying out for football as a pastime and stress reliever. Though it was strange to write down his feelings at first—as typically, men (black men especially) are not expected to do those kinds of things. In fact, for the first few days, Kevon kept this activity private, as he feared the other students might ridicule and marginalize him more. However, the more he practiced journaling, the more he was able to confront his feelings by writing them down. Journaling even gave Kevon much-needed feelings of catharsis from the deep-seated anger he harbored. After a few weeks, Kevon decided to also try out for the football team. He had struggled with thinking he was not good enough as he felt like he was "not being accepted by his own people". This was his way of proving he was good enough.

Through regular journaling, Kevon was able to channel his anger and negative thoughts onto paper and keep them down, quieted, at least until the next time they crept in again. By also finding an activity he enjoyed (football), he managed to use his time at practice to focus on what he enjoyed.

5

COGNITIVE DEFUSION

What you feed your mind, will lead your life.

— KEMI SOGUNLE

O kay, before you start worrying about the technical term and how it is probably from a therapy lesson, consider the following exercise: Put your hands on your lap, side-by-side like they are two pages in a book. In this exercise, your hands represent your thoughts, especially those repetitive, negative ones. Now slowly bring your hands up to your face, until they are almost touching your face and covering your eyes, so that you can only see through the gaps in your fingers. Notice how hard it is to see anything else besides your hands. You are entangled by them. You are removed and disconnected from your environment with very little information getting in. Now, imagine what it would be like to go around like this, all day. Think about how difficult it would be to be productive or respond to life's challenges. This is what we meant by fusion–which is the opposite of cognitive defusion.

Now, slowly lower your hands and put them back onto your lap. Do you notice what happens as the space between you and your hands (thoughts) increases? Do you notice what happens between you and the room; how much more information is coming in and how much easier it becomes to engage the world and become productive? Keep in mind that your hands (thoughts) have not disappeared and that they are still sitting right there. And if there is anything useful and productive you can do with them, by all means, use them! If not, just let them sit there. When we get some space from our problematic thoughts, we can begin to see more clearly and become flexible in our behavior. That is how cognitive defusion works.

Just like that exercise, cognitive defusion trains you to know how to notice your thoughts and identify the negative ones. When you find yourself stuck in a negative thought loop, it can be very difficult to clearly see the bigger picture. You might even be frustrated as you struggle to identify your thoughts as you realize how they are affecting you. But when you allow your mind to pull away and identify the negative thoughts, you can begin to reframe them in a positive way. So now that you have a better idea of the concept of cognitive defusion in theory, you may wonder what it looks like in practice? Well, here's an example:

Najee, 26, who has struggled with depression and anxiety for over eight years, often finds himself thinking: *"Crap! I'm such a loser!"* Other times he thinks: *"Why am I always so anxious?"* Najee repeatedly allows these thoughts to consume him as they solidify his *truths* and fuel his feelings of depression and anxiety. Because Najee has continually told himself that he is a loser or that he is not good enough, that has become his truth. Because of this, Najee found himself struggling with presentations at work and his productivity significantly dropped.

But what if Najee had learned about cognitive defusion? This would have helped him quiet his negative thoughts and helped him regain his confidence and productivity. How would cognitive defusion help him change his feelings about himself? Therapists who teach cognitive defusion techniques to their patients often encourage them to shift their thinking. In Najee's case, for example, instead of telling himself, for example, *"I guess I'm only telling myself that I'm a loser,"* he can start stretching his arms and realize, *"I'm only experiencing anxiety at this moment".* When you practice cognitive defusion, you can identify that you *do* have a choice and hold the power to change what they think and that their feelings are only a temporary experience.

Cognitive defusion (also known as deliteralization) is described as a technique typically used in Acceptance and Commitment Therapy to help people deal with unpleasant or unhelpful thoughts and feelings (Washington Center for Cognitive Therapy, 2014). Because such thoughts serve no purpose and are just going to bring your mood all the way down, cognitive defusion can be a useful technique for people with depression and anxiety. It involves creating space between ourselves, and our thoughts and feelings so that they have less of a hold over us.

Another metaphor typically used in explaining cognitive defusion is "Passengers on the Bus" (Washington Center for Cognitive Therapy, 2014). In this exercise, picture yourself as a driver on a bus full of passengers. In this case, think of your life's journey like driving this bus. You are in charge, right? Now imagine there are passengers on this bus, and as you move along, you are picking up additional passengers. Imagine these passengers as your thoughts, feelings, and memories. Some of these passengers (thoughts) are quite lovely.

For example, one could be, *"I have a great partner,"* or *"I have a rewarding job"*. But the others? Not as pleasant. In fact, many of them can be thoroughly obnoxious, like: *"Don't do it! You'll make a fool of yourself"*, *"Deep down, you know you're just not good enough"*, *"Why bother?"* or *"No one really knows how to love you."* These passengers do not hesitate to speak up and criticize you. In addition, they even start telling you how to drive! *"Turn right here, pull over, slow down, speed up!"* As the bus driver, what do you do? Well, you can either choose to argue with them or tell them to hush down, right? You could even stop the bus and either try to reason with them or kick them off! But notice, if you do this, then you are no longer driving the bus anymore. You have stopped in order to deal with them (and there can be a lot of them, some are even pretty strong). Chances are—instead of yielding to reason—they will likely tell you what to do, or else they might have to get right in your face. This can become very problematic as you are stuck on the side of your life journey trying to negotiate or eliminate negative thoughts (passengers).

The opposite of cognitive defusion, known as cognitive fusion, is when you find yourself looking at life from the lenses and perspective of your thoughts. What this means is that you become stuck to your thoughts and believe everything that comes into your head without even questioning or challenging it. When you get fused or hooked to the strong negative beliefs about yourself, it can bring you suffering and emotional unrest. You start to contort into painful shapes (for most of your life) because you have boxed yourself in with negative beliefs like: *"I'm only going to be respected and loveable if I succeed in life"*. You may find yourself holding onto these beliefs so much that you forget they are just beliefs! They are not facts or the truth! But because you've conditioned yourself to these thoughts and beliefs, you begin to think they are 100% true. In fact, you may even get annoyed if people question them.

Consider the following illustration of how a person can be fused with her thoughts and color her world in a negative way:

Andrea, a 31-year-old woman who suffered from social anxiety disorder (SAD), found it difficult to hang out with friends. Once, at a party, where she was with her friends from work, she started feeling really anxious. While talking with a group of her work colleagues, she would try to make jokes to ease her anxiety. Sometimes, when she didn't get an animated response, she would start to worry afterwards whether she said the wrong thing or hurt someone's feelings. Other times when a group of friends would split up and move over to the grill or gazebo, she would feel terrified and panic because she would not know which group to go with. Because Andrea was aware that she would get negative thoughts, she would find herself staring into space and drifting off, as an internal battle to fight those negative thoughts ensued in her head. *"Oh, my gosh, why am I feeling this way again"*, she would think—then almost immediately challenge that by telling herself, *"What is wrong with you? Quit feeling anxious and enjoy this party, girl!"*. Andrea would do this dance every time she found herself feeling anxious in a social setting. On occasions when she failed to win the battle with her thoughts, she would feel overwhelmed and decide to leave the party instead.

In this example, we realize that Andrea was fused with her thoughts in two ways.

The first is that she was caught up in fighting her negative thoughts to make them go away. She ended up using all her mental energy fighting her thoughts instead of trying to have a good time and enjoy the party (something she had been wanting for a long time).

The second way is that Andrea always believed that in a social setting, she might hurt or offend someone by saying the wrong thing. In all her experiences, she would always overthink interactions and conversations, and worry that she may have said something that left someone bothered and uncomfortable. She dreaded having to deal with the drama and awkwardness that would follow if this happened.

Without realizing it, Andrea had made a rule that she would not let any of her interactions leave anyone feeling bad. In fact, Andrea struggled with expressing how she truly felt if she believed it would hurt someone's feelings. As a result, it kept her from enjoying and expressing her own feelings.

Just like in Andrea's case, when you believe all the things you think, without questioning or noticing them, it can keep you from enjoying your life and focusing on your productivity. The key to overcoming this, however, is by learning to look *at* your thoughts instead of *through* your thoughts. Much like the exercise you did earlier, when you look through your thoughts, you see the world in the negative way you think. When your negative thoughts are the only things in front of you, and when they cover your perspective, you struggle with accepting any other truth or perspective. But when you look *at* your thoughts, you are able to realize how unhelpful and untrue your thoughts can be.

If Andrea looked *at* her thoughts instead of through them, she would have been able to realize that she cannot control how people will think, feel, or react to the things she says, no matter *how* careful she is. If she had stopped looking through her thoughts, it would have helped her feel less anxious, and she would have been able to enjoy the party.

When you begin looking at your thoughts instead of through them, you will be able to see how these thoughts may be affecting you and your behavior. Defusing yourself from negative thoughts and beliefs can become a moment of blessed relief– like when you take off a pair of shoes that are one size too small or when you finally remove your bra after a long day!

The key moment in your recovery from depression and social anxiety can be the switch from strongly held beliefs, such as, *"No one likes me because I am broken,"* to the realization, *"This is actually the belief that is causing me to struggle"*. It can be like becoming lucid in a dream —when you realize, *"Aaaah, I see. I am doing this to myself"*.

TECHNIQUES ON OVERCOMING ANXIETY AND NEGATIVE THINKING USING COGNITIVE DEFUSION

1. Write down or say out loud all the thoughts that run through your mind. For example, you may already start to wonder how this will help or that it is silly. Write that too! After all, it is a thought. Now, when you are done, add the words **"I notice that I am thinking..."**

Adding this phrase to your repetitive negative thoughts will allow you to notice how you have been seeing the world through your thoughts. It will also show you the kind of relationship you have with these thoughts.

2. **Label your thoughts**. You can put them into two categories, namely useful and unhelpful.

3. Come up with **short phrases for your repetitive, negative thoughts**. For example, *"There's my 'I'm incompetent' thought"* or *"There goes my 'negative nature' again"*.

4. The next time you notice a very negative thought creeping up on you, say it to yourself, write it down, and then **read it out in a silly voice**, like Daffy Duck or Goofy. Read it out loud, over and over. This will remind you that they are just words and not reality. Whenever you hear these negative thoughts try to come back, always play them back in the same ridiculous voice.

5. Write down on a piece of paper a negative thought or belief that you feel is holding you back. Then take that piece of paper, fold or scrunch it up, take it to the toilet, and **flush it** down. As you flush, say to yourself out loud: *"This is a negative belief/thought and because it serves me no purpose, I am letting it go"*.

6

PRACTICING GRATITUDE

Gratitude unlocks the fullness of life. It turns what we have into enough, and more. It turns denial into acceptance, chaos to order, confusion to clarity. It can turn a meal into a feast, a house into a home, a stranger into a friend.

— MELODY BEATTIE

D id you know that gratitude has been proven to make you feel happier and more positive in your life while eliminating the feelings of loneliness and isolation? It is true. Although science has just recently caught up to this fact, Buddhist monks have known about it for decades!

Perhaps one of the first images that come to mind when you hear the word "gratitude" or the phrase "being thankful" is the tradition of Thanksgiving. During this holiday, friends and family gather around and celebrate all the things they are thankful for. While this is a great way to show appreciation for the people in your life, it is also a good way to reflect on the things we often overlook and take for granted.

In the famous words of Ferris Bueller: "Life moves pretty fast. If you don't stop and look around once in a while, you could miss it." It can be easy to get over-whelmed in the fast lane and be left feeling anxious and more stressed. This can make it all the more difficult to pause and just show appreciation for the good things in your life. Often, we get so caught up in stressing about the things we do not have and all the things we want, while neglecting the things we do have. Yet, we forget that we have so many other things to be grateful for.

People who experience anxiety and stress can attest to finding themselves often worrying about the future and whether or not they will get what they want or if things will work in their favor. But as ancient wisdom tells us: *"A life well lived is one of gratitude and thankfulness."*

The word gratitude is derived from the Latin word *gratia*, which means grace, graciousness, or gratefulness —depending on the context (Miller, 2016). In many ways, gratitude encompasses all of these meanings. Being grateful means having a sincere appreciation for what you have, whether it is tangible or intangible. In this process, individuals typically recognize that the source of that goodness lies, at least partially, beyond themselves. As a result, when you are grateful, you are able to connect to something larger than yourself— whether it is to other people, nature, or a higher power.

Practicing gratitude has been proven to be an effective way of improving mental health and contributing to overall wellness and happiness. Gratitude can help you feel more positive emotions, look forward to good experiences, improve your mental and emotional health, deal with anxiety, and build strong relationships. Practicing gratitude on a daily basis can also be a great way of silencing your negative emotions and thoughts.

As mentioned, one of the many characteristics of anxiety is worry. Whether you find yourself worrying about the future, or questioning your individual capability to get something done, anxiety (accompanied by stress) can leave you crippled with low self-esteem, feelings of unworthiness, and even self-loathing. You start beating yourself up thinking, *"Nothing good ever happens to me,"* or *"I'm never going to do this"*. But we never seem to pause and think, *"Hold on, what about all the things I have done?"* or *"What about all those good things that have happened to me?".*

One of the hindrances or obstacles that restrict us from seeing things from such an angle is the tunnel vision of *right now.* We get so caught up thinking and focusing on our worries in the moment (or those yet to come) that we forget about all the other good things that have come to us and the achievements we have accomplished.

For example, have you ever found yourself worrying about a situation that did not end well for you? Or, better yet, a job interview that you did not get? When you think about it with an obstructed tunnel view, all you can see are the negative thoughts: *"I can't believe I didn't get that job!"* You could choose to focus on that, OR you could think: *"At least I got an interview. Clearly, I must have something worth checking out,"* or *"I'm happy that they called me for an interview at least. It must mean they saw some potential. I just need to improve my CV or skillset".* When you think this way or show gratitude in such a situation, it will leave you feeling more motivated.

Most people think practicing gratitude means being thankful for the *big things* in your life—having a good job or a successful career, stability, or a loving wife and family. Rightly so, these are all things we ought to be grateful for. However, gratitude does not have to be reserved for these big things in your life. The habit of being thankful can (and should) start with appreciating *every* good thing in your life and recognizing that there is nothing that is too small to be grateful for. Even if it is as simple as appreciating the clear, sunny weather or how quickly your courier delivered your package last Thursday, it is important you leave nothing out when practicing your gratitude.

When you continuously practice living your life with gratitude, you begin to notice the little wins—like when the bus shows up on time, a stranger compliments you, or when the sun greets you in the morning by shining through your window when you wake up.

This may seem silly at first when you start practicing it, but the more you do it (especially with the smaller things), the more you begin to realize how good you have it. Practicing gratitude can be a game-changer. Each of these small moments strings together to create a web of well-being that, over time, strengthens your ability to deflect your negative thoughts and emotions, anxiety and stress. Like Oprah Winfrey once said: "Be thankful for what you have; you'll end up having more. If you concentrate on what you don't have, you will never, ever have enough."

Because of the differences in our fortunes and experiences, our thankfulness can look different. There are some universal things we can be grateful for, for example being alive, surrounded by caring friends and family, or just having a roof over our heads. But because our experiences are different, some of the things you are grateful for may seem trivial to another. While you may be grateful for having a good job or nice house, someone is simply grateful that they had a decent meal today or that they have clothes on their back.

Understanding and recognizing that sometimes our worries and anxieties pale in comparison to other people's situations can be a great way to realize the things we may take for granted. This does not mean you are discarding how you may feel or trivializing it. It just simply means that sometimes your worries and fears are things you can overcome because of the opportunities you have.

Here is an exercise for you get a better understanding:

The View from Above: This is actually an exercise derived from ancient Greek philosophy. Think of yourself and your situation (the worries that you have). Then picture yourself zooming out and looking at it from the sky. Picture your house and the street you live on. Then zoom out further and picture the city and the country underneath the clouds. Then zoom out even further and picture the continent you are on, and the

Earth spinning round. Then zoom out again and picture the solar system, and then the whole galaxy of the Milky Way, and the thousands and thousands of galaxies, containing billions and billions of stars and planets. With the limitless expanse of the universe, glittering with light and energy, pause and ask yourself: *"What was I getting so worked up about?"*

As mentioned, by no means is this exercise meant to sideline your emotions, thoughts and feelings. Instead, this exercise is designed to help you challenge your negative thoughts and emotions (such as feelings of worry), and make you realize that you are a small but significant piece in a much bigger puzzle.

Consider the following example:

On a recent trip to Bangkok, Linda and her husband climbed to a monastery and set up camp at 11 500 feet. The air was clean, and the views were breathtaking. And yet, as the sun went down to create a beautiful orangish-red outline, all Linda could think about was her freezing hands and feet. As she huddled around the fire with her husband and other campers, all Linda wanted was to climb into her sleeping bag, warm herself up, and go to sleep. With the temperatures having dropped to just below zero, any joy she had become overshadowed by her chattering teeth.

Their guide, on the other hand, looked impervious to the cold. All he wore was a traditional knee-length robe that ties at the waist—and yet there Linda was, bundled up in a puffer jacket and struggling with the cold. Linda asked the man if he was cold, and he said that he was *grateful* to be able to camp on this sacred site. Linda could not believe her guide's answer, so she kept questioning him. She truly could not understand how he was able to ignore the bone-chilling cold in a robe that looked barely warm. She asked the man if he did not want a warmer jacket. His reply humbled Linda. *"Rather than focusing on what I do not have, I choose to focus on what I do have. I am lucky to have this fire. I am lucky to have this job, I am lucky to have a tent, and I am lucky to have your company."* At that moment, Linda realized that her guide had just shared a very important key to happiness.

Much like in Linda's case, when you focus on your blessings, it allows you to celebrate the present moment and focus your attention on the good instead of the bad. Our nature as humans is to want what we do not have; focusing on the negatives instead of celebrating the things we do have and all the positives.

Linda and her husband had spent months planning a trip, but instead of enjoying her excursion, she had spent hours complaining about the heat and later about the cold. But as she listened to her guide share his contagious feelings of gratitude, Linda's attitude changed, and she began to think about her blessings. Linda went on to relax and enjoy the nature and stillness of the night. She looked up into the night sky and began to focus on the stars, which she realized could not really be enjoyed living in the city.

Here's the thing: being grateful has the power to block out negative thoughts and emotions. You can't really pay attention to what is going well, or the things you have, if you let your mind pay attention to what you don't have, or what is going wrong.

Practicing gratitude can help you refocus and eliminate negative thoughts that can bring your mood down and leave you feeling worthless or incompetent. And, although it may feel contrived at first, practicing gratefulness allows your mental state to grow stronger.

Building your capacity for gratitude is not difficult at all. It just requires daily practice. The more you can bring your attention to things you feel grateful for (no matter how small), the more you'll notice additional things to be grateful for! So, to help you begin your gratitude journey and relieve yourself of some stress, anxiety and negativity, here are some techniques to help you practice more gratitude in your daily life.

TECHNIQUES TO PRACTICE GRATITUDE AND ELIMINATE NEGATIVITY

1. Keep a Gratitude Journal: This is a great way to keep track of the things you are grateful for. It is also a good way to remind yourself of the good things you have. Start by writing, in no particular order, *everything* you can think of that you are grateful for—no matter how small. Make this a daily practice any chance you get—be it when you wake up or before you sleep. Make sure your journal is portable because you are going to need it for whenever your negative thoughts creep up on you. When this happens, you can open it up to any entry and remind yourself of the gifts, grace, and good things you have. Even when you are not experiencing any negative thoughts, just set aside time on a daily basis to go through your journal. The entries of gratitude for *ordinary events* (such as, *waking up in the morning*), personal attributes, or valued relationships in your life will give you the ability to interweave a lifetime theme of gratefulness and contentment.

2. Practice Mindfulness: If you do not enjoy writing, you can try mindfulness instead. Choose a daily time and think of five to ten things you are grateful for. You need to picture these things in your mind as you think of them. Then say them out loud (or softly, if you feel awkward about doing it in front of other people). When you do this every day, it will rewire your brain, which will become naturally more grateful. You will start feeling happier every time you do this. It only takes eight weeks of mindfulness practice for a person to start showing a change in brain patterns. Remember, your brain is a powerful tool, and training it to become involuntarily grateful will be a great way to ensure that your mind focuses on the positivity in your life.

3. Remember the Bad: While you are not meant to stay in this state, reminding yourself of how far you have come, and the things you have overcome, can be a great way to appreciate where you are now. Take one to two minutes (time yourself) to think about the hard times you have experienced in your past. You can write them down or say them out loud. Next, set up an explicit contrast in your mind for each bad time. It does not have to be directly related. For example, *"I did not get that promotion I wanted"*, then contrast it with, *"I am grateful for my kids"*. Recognizing the bad experiences can make you appreciate the good things even more. When you realize that all the bad things that have happened have led you to where you can now appreciate the things you have, it can really leave you feeling all the more thankful. Contrasting is the perfect ground for gratefulness.

4. Volunteer for a Cause or Charity: For some people, a good way to cultivate more gratitude is by giving back to others in their local community. Not only does volunteering make you feel more grateful for the things that you may take for granted, but it also gives you a sense of purpose. Find a charitable organization, an elderly home, or a homeless shelter and commit your time for a few hours each week. Talk to the people you see there. Listen to their stories and take in their advice (if they give it). You will begin to realize that your problems may pale in comparison to theirs. This will make you more grateful for the things you have and you can stop worrying so much about tomorrow's uncertainties. In other words: helping others will help you!

5. Spend Time with Loved Ones: If you are struggling with feeling gratitude in the moment, go spend time with your friends and family. Not only will it bring you closer to them, but it will also give you a chance to practice your acts of gratitude on the people you care about most. Start small. For instance, when you are speaking to someone, listen intently instead of just waiting for your chance to speak. You can also practice complimenting their new shoes or outfit.

6. Replace Those Complaints with Gratitude: When you find yourself focusing on what you think you are lacking, replace those negative thoughts with things you are grateful for. This may sound familiar to technique number 3, but the difference is that this can be negative thoughts about your current situation or worries about the future. For example, if you find yourself thinking, *"I wish my car was nicer"*, *"I wish I had a bigger house"* or *"If only I had more money"*, replace it with *"I'm grateful I have a car"* or *"I'm thankful for having a roof over my head"*.

7

ELIMINATE TOO MANY CHOICES

If you chase two rabbits, both will escape.

— UNKNOWN AUTHOR

Have you ever found yourself overthinking a decision because there are just too many choices or options? One of the key issues people who struggle with anxiety and overthinking have often dealt with is making a decision in the face of many options. While it is quite normal for anyone to take time in deciding what pizza they would like to order or which flavor ice-cream to try, overthinkers find it extremely difficult to make a decision with a plethora of options laid out for them. In cases where a decision requires a timely response, people who suffer from overthinking can lose out on opportunities because they fail to make a choice soon enough.

When you struggle with making decisions in the face of many choices, it can really become difficult to become confident in your decision-making. You start to over-think every choice, weighing the pros and cons of each choice while the timer continues to run down. In some cases, it may even be a simple choice that you may need to make. For example, it has been a long-running joke that most women have difficulty deciding what they want to wear. Despite this only being a stereotype, many people do struggle with the confidence of making a decision as they overthink their options.

Understandably, it can be very difficult to make certain decisions on a whim. For example, when you are looking to buy a new television or washing machine, you cannot be expected to simply pick out the first one you see as soon as you walk into the store. You will likely check each appliance's specifications and brand and weigh your choices against each other. This may take some time, and you may even want to think about it while you shop for other things in the store.

This is normal and typically happens with most people. Whether you do your research on the internet by reading reviews first or watching YouTube review videos, you take ample time to gather enough information to make a sound decision with which you are both comfortable and happy.

When you take time to make a decision on an *expensive, big, or technical* product, this is known as a "high involvement purchase" (Nayeem & Casidy, 2013). With a high-involvement purchase, you will typically go through an extensive thought process and consider a lot of variables before finally making your final decision. If you have ever bought a car at a dealership, you will naturally go through such an extensive thought process. This does not make you an overthinker, it just makes you careful and considerate of your choice.

The reason why we lament and mull over a decision that includes a high-involvement product is pretty straightforward and simple. Because the product we are buying is typically an expensive one, it would be a big disappointment if it didn't meet our expectations. In addition, if we made a *bad choice,* it can knock our confidence in making any future decisions so quickly.

When you experience these feelings after making a purchase that you regret, this is known as "post-purchase dissonance" (Bhasin, 2019). Post-purchase dissonance can also happen even with smaller products that require less extensive research and quicker decision-making.

For example, Kesha was looking at purchasing a home-coming dress. Because of the pandemic, most stores had moved to virtual sales and because of her limited resources, she wanted to see if she could score a better deal online. In her mind, Kesha wanted an affordable dress that still had enough *pazazz and glam* to look stunning. Kesha scoured the different online stores and boutiques she could find, hoping to find the perfect dress.

Finally, on an Instagram boutique, Kesha found *the* dress. She quickly ordered it in her size as she was worried it would sell out. After a few days, it arrived on her doorstep and like a kid in a toy store, she was buzzing with excitement. She scurried upstairs and opened the box to try on her new dress. To her horror, the quality of the dress was nowhere near the standard it indicated! For the money she had paid, Kesha was left very disappointed and angry at herself for not doing research on the vendor and finding reviews.

We've all made some *regrettable decisions* in the past that have led to such post-purchase dissonance. This may not only leave you with feelings of regret and disappointment, but you can start to lose confidence in your ability to make sound decisions. While post-purchase dissonance typically occurs even in the absence of a variety of options, the availability of choices can make your decision all the more difficult (Di Schiena *et. al.*, 2013).

Usually, in the face of many decisions, a person will usually take their time and weigh their options. However, when you find your life and confidence are disrupted by too many options, it is known as "choice paralysis". Though it is true that choice is the variety and spice of life, and is an essential part of everyday living, having more choice is not always a good thing and can be quite stressful.

For instance, Jack has scored himself a date with Amy after crushing on her for a few months. He would like to take her to a nice restaurant that is within his budget. He does not want to take her to a restaurant that is *tacky* or cheap, like a fast-food restaurant. He prefers something classier with a *sophisticated* ambiance. After conducting his research, Jack has found four restaurants that fit his budget. Two of them have a wide menu (in case she is allergic or intolerant to some foods), and both have the ambiance he is looking for, but they are located much further away than he would prefer. The other two have a slightly lesser appeal but are located much closer to his area. Jack is now burdened with the stress of deciding which restaurant to pick for his date. He would obviously like to make a very good impression, but now he cannot even decide which restaurant to go to. This leads him to become increasingly stressed and might jeopardize his confidence for the rest of the date as he might find himself second-guessing his choice.

If you have ever experienced something similar, or stood in the aisle of a supermarket unable to decide between 12 different flavors of ice cream, then you suffer from choice paralysis. Instead of being able to confidently decide, you spend so much time over-thinking your choices and sometimes end up not coming to any decision at all.

If you struggle with anxiety and overthinking, the more choices presented in front of you, the harder it can become to make a decision. In addition, when choices become more complex or important, the amount of mental energy we use in trying to analyze also increases. This is often termed "analysis paralysis". This certainly does not help in silencing your mind.

In fact, having to make a choice in the face of many options (especially the complex and important ones) can create negative emotions and thoughts that can lead to decision fatigue or anxiety procrastination. You begin to delay your decision because you are worried that you will make the wrong one. In many cases, even if you end up making a choice, decision paralysis can leave you so exhausted that you do not have any energy left to carry out the action itself.

Understanding choice paralysis is crucial because in cases where it leads to anxiety and procrastination, it can derail our productivity. When you are supposed to do two or more important things but find it difficult to know which to start first, there is a chance you may end up not starting at all!

Here is a very interesting study to help you understand. There is a very famous collection of experiments involving jam and choice that was conducted to determine the impact of choice paralysis.

In the 1980s, Consumer Reports brought together a panel of taste palette experts to judge which strawberry jam—out of 45 choices—tasted the best. They were scored by these experts based on a variety of characteristics, including spreadability and fruitiness. The list of final choices was concluded. A few years later, a psychologist named Timothy Wilson decided to replicate the experiment to see if students would pick the same jams as the experts. He randomly picked five of the jams from the list, and had students rank them after tasting. Surprisingly, the students highly agreed with the expert's choices. They thought: *"We're as good as the experts in taste testing!"*

However, Wilson then asked a second group of students to pick their favorites, using all 45 original jams, instead of the random selection of five, and think about *why* they chose them. This time there were only a few who agreed with the expert's choices! (Wilson & Schooler, 1991) The experiment, therefore, concluded the following: When a person has more choices, their decision-making is worsened.

You may ask: *"But won't having more options make me happier in the long run?"* The paradox in decision paralysis is not just about the difficulty in making a choice. More importantly, a person may spend time thinking about the choices they did not make, instead of being content with the ones they did. The more choices, the more likely you may feel like you *missed out*. You find yourself wondering: "What if I had chosen this instead of that?"

This circles back to the previous chapter about learning to be grateful. You end up thinking about what you could have had instead of focusing on what you *do* have —which is not very ideal when you think about life-changing decisions, like which major to study in college, or what job to take. You can imagine how unhappy and even depressed you could become if you chose the wrong career path. You would be miserable!

If you often find yourself faced with the anxiety of choosing a meal for dinner when presented with a variety of options or stressed out over which flavor of yogurt to try, you know how mentally draining it can be. Luckily, there are a few techniques you can follow to reduce decision paralysis, and learn how to stop procrastination from derailing your productivity.

TECHNIQUES TO ELIMINATE CHOICE PARALYSIS

1. Minimize Your Options: When faced with the decision of choosing a spice or drink, for example, insist on keeping your options to a minimum. We like having a variety of choices because it feels luxurious and it gives the feeling that we can change our minds later, in case we make the wrong decision. But most times, changing your decision will only leave you feeling negative (self-blame) and knock your confidence. When you limit your options to things you are comfortable or confident with, then your decisions will lead to less regret.

Consider the example of Summer, who has a choice of about 13 salad dressings at her local supermarket. Out of the 13, she had only tried four—two of which she had only tried because they were in her parents' fridge. As Summer tried to buy another type of dressing, she became overwhelmed. She spent 20 minutes looking at bottles trying to figure out which would taste the best. She finally bought one that looked tasty, took it home and realized it tasted awful. She started to think of how she had wasted her money and should have just gone with the ginger miso salad dressing instead. While this was a small thing, she could not stop thinking how stupid she was for making such a decision.

When you **limit your options to at most four or five choices**, your decision-making can become more satisfying with less regret, stress and anxiety. You can find freedom in limiting your own choices. As they say, less is more!

2. Improve Self-Confidence: Before you think, *"Well, wait, would it not be better to explore more options?"* or *"Surely it's restrictive to be caged in by your choices,"* ask yourself if your confidence can allow you to try something new without feeling bad if it does not work out? The truth is very few people do. So, the key to expanding your freedom of choice is to improve your self-confidence first. Practice thinking back to decisions you made *blindly* that turned out well and remind yourself that it is okay to make mistakes. Do this every day and look at every opportunity to make a new decision as just an opportunity to learn more about yourself, instead of a potential for failure.

3. Put a Limit On Your Decision-Making Timeline:
As previously discussed, there may be situations that
will require extensive research before making a decision. This means your decision-making may take
longer than usual. However, prolonged decision-
making can be problematic. When you practice putting
a timeline on your decision-making you can start to
make decisions without having to overthink them. For
example, if you have to choose a pizza for dinner, give
yourself five minutes to make a decision. Take your
phone and put a timer on it! It can actually be a fun way
to make a decision if you let it. And in case you might
worry about how this will only increase your anxiety,
have a look at the next technique.

4. Trust Your Gut: Instincts usually relate less to logic
and more to lived experience and emotions. If you
normally rely on research and logical reasoning when
making decisions, then you may feel a little uneasy
about letting your feelings guide important decisions.
Start with small decisions and build that trust. For
example, if you feel like trying out a new flavor of ice
cream or electronic brand, trust what your gut is telling
you. Close your eyes and think about how the product
or ice cream flavor you want makes you feel. Follow
your instincts!

5. Talk to Four People: Why four people, you wonder? Well, should you still feel reluctant about your decision and not completely trust your gut, you can get an opinion from other people. When you consult one person or three, they may have conflicting opinions- and coupled with yours, you may find yourself in a stalemate. For example, if you are deciding on a watch to buy and you have two options, you may take a picture and send it to three of your friends to help you decide. Two of them may think 'watch A' looks better, while you and the other friend believe 'watch B' suits you better. This could leave you frustrated. So, in order to break the stalemate, you can talk to four people instead. The majority of choices versus your gut may help make your decision easier. Remember, decision-making can also be a team effort! And in some situations, you will need help.

6. Practice Acceptance: Suppose you are struggling to decide on the perfect location for your first date. Take a moment to remind yourself that there are a lot of great locations but not necessarily one *perfect spot*. Now, take ONE minute (strictly one minute!) and choose a location from the places that you have shortlisted, no matter how uneasy this makes you feel. There! You are done! Now, comes the last part: accepting your choice. Even if the place you picked has some things you do not particularly like and your date does not go flawlessly, it is okay. Again, this can only be achieved once you start practicing gratitude! Plus, maybe you'll have a funny story to share afterward!

7. Get Comfortable with Uncertainty: Much like the technique before, understanding that it is not possible to plan for every outcome or possibility is a great way to eliminate your anxiety. Always find a time every day to remind yourself (for at least two minutes) that life is full of unknowns and that even though making one choice will prevent you from knowing the outcome of the other choices, that *is* how life works. Sure, uncertainty can make you very anxious. It can even be scary. But no one knows how ALL decisions would turn out in the end. That is why it is important that you trust your instincts, improve your confidence and practice gratitude. Doing this will help you achieve the serenity to accept the things you cannot change, give you the confidence to change the things you can change, and the gratitude to live one day at a time, taking this world as it is and not as you would have it.

Some examples:

- When you cannot decide on what to eat for dinner: Do a meal prep or have a three-meal rotation. You are welcome to add different ingredients to spruce up the dishes.

- Unsure what to wear to work: Create a uniform! Or coordinate your wardrobe. Find what goes best with what and stick to that until you are confident enough to switch things up.
- Deciding which restaurants to order from or go to: Create a list of your top 10 places on your phone in descending order—from most favorite to least preferred.

8

KNOW YOUR TRIGGERS

> *You cannot always control what goes on outside,*
> *but you can always control what goes on inside.*
>
> — WAYNE DYER

Finding your "triggers" ties into you knowing when you are overthinking or when you are stressed and anxious. While identifying *when* you become anxious or stressed is important, it presents a more reactionary approach rather than a proactive one.

You will typically be able to identify when you become stressed or anxious because of how it may make you feel or how your body may react. However, when this happens it requires techniques to combat it when it happens. But have you ever wondered if there was something you could do *before* anxiety or stress affects you? Have you found yourself thinking, *"Ugh, I hate being this anxious".*

In addition to knowing your symptoms, it is beneficial to your peace of mind to know your triggers. People who suffer from anxiety can attest to feeling *attacked* or *jumped* when their anxiety strikes. Because anxiety catches you off guard it can be very difficult to always know what causes it. And because you have no idea why you are suddenly feeling so anxious, you may start feeling even more anxious and stressed! This only perpetuates the cycle, and you may be stuck in the loop for a while.

Rose knew she struggled with anxiety after her 22nd birthday when she had an anxiety attack in the middle of a day at work. For months she struggled to understand why she would get *random* anxiety attacks when she had done all her tasks and her life seemed to be going well. These attacks continued happening to her. She would be going about her day when all of a sudden, she would feel a pang of anxiety–and then a burst. Then a wave. She realized a pattern in the symptoms, occurring almost every time after a certain time of day. Unbeknownst to her, she was simply drinking too much coffee! Her daily routine involved a coffee run before work and another one in the middle of the morning. While Rose was aware of her anxiety symptoms (and was managing them, in terms of controlling them as they happen), she wondered what she was doing wrong that kept triggering them. After deciding to track her routine and ease up on the caffeine, Rose started to notice that her anxiety attacks became fewer and fewer each week.

If you have found yourself in a similar position, then you appreciate how important it can be to know your triggers. When you become aware of the things that trigger your anxieties and stress, you put yourself in a prime position to be able to avoid them and control your anxiety before it happens. The moment Rose realized something may be triggering her anxiety, she tried finding a pattern by pausing and tracking her routine. *"Is there anything I just read?", "What did I just see?"* or *"Did I hear something unusual?"* You may be surprised to find out that some of your triggers are coming from very small things that you can actually control.

Another example is Carlos, who was an intern at a marketing firm. Because Carlos was an intern who wanted to make a mark in his industry, he was always overthinking his work. Because he wanted to learn and do his best to show his potential, Carlos always strived to create the most perfect presentations. His manager often communicated through the team's Slack app.

Whenever there was a notice or announcement, the manager would relay it through the app for convenience. Because feedback on presentations and general work performance was also communicated through the app, it made Carlos very anxious when he presented his work and awaited feedback. Every ping on a phone (even when it is not his) would make him sweat. Carlos had not realized that in his struggle to become the best intern, he had unknowingly paved the way for a pattern and habit to form...one where any ping would trigger his anxiety.

Then there's Tanerelle, who struggled with fitting in at her high school. Her peers always wore the trendiest of clothes, hairstyles, and makeup. She could not afford such expensive luxuries, and every time she fantasized about the things she would buy or have when she got money, she would feel stressed. What's more, when she would open her Instagram, her feed would be filled with people in trendy clothes and hairstyles. While it can be much easier for a person like Tanerelle to know her trigger, most people are unaware that such an activity can cause stress and anxiety. It becomes an unconscious trigger because it happens without you realizing it.

In severe cases, anxiety and stress triggers can worsen symptoms to the point of making you suffer a panic attack. Panic attacks are sudden episodes of severe and debilitating fear (Hull, 2021). When you have a panic attack, it can be very terrifying as you may even feel like the world is closing in on you, and you are about to die. These feelings of extreme anxiety and panic can interrupt your daily life and productivity and can be very hard to control. In addition, they are often out of proportion to the actual danger and can often last a while.

You may have become so used to anxiety that you do not notice it in yourself. You feel restless, tingling sensations, irritability, tightness in your chest, insomnia, digestive issues, or feeling like your throat is closing, and you cannot breathe. Those are all just *signs* of panic and not necessarily triggers. Identifying what *triggers* these signs is what can help you calm your mind by nipping it in the bud.

Knowing what causes your anxiety or stress is a good way to move past fear and live more freely. Identifying and dealing with anxiety triggers sooner rather than later can be beneficial in helping you manage your anxiety. Typically, when something triggers your anxiety, and you start experiencing severe emotions as a result, most people resort to self-care activities to reduce their anxiety (Ehrenfeld, 2019). Once the anxiety kicks in, that is when you usually adopt some of the coping mechanisms previously discussed—such as distraction and positive reframing. But when you know what causes this anxiety or stress, it can be an advantage as you gain an upper hand.

You might already have a general idea of what bothers you most, such as your health, finances or crowds. Before you can become specific, you may want to know the types of anxiety disorders, to learn how to identify the triggers and avoid them. Here are some common anxiety disorders that exist as outlined by the Mayo Clinic (2018a):

- **Panic Attacks:** This type of anxiety involves repeated episodes of sudden and intense feelings of anxiety, fear, and/or terror that can increase within minutes. Common symptoms may include shortness of breath, tightness in the chest, feelings of impending doom, or a rapid pounding heart (heart palpitations). Sometimes even during a panic attack, you may start worrying about the fact that you are having a panic attack, which only intensifies your symptoms.
- **Generalized Anxiety Disorder**: This is perhaps the most common form of anxiety. It includes persistent and excessive worry about activities or events— even ordinary ones that

have not happened yet. Typically, the worry is out of proportion to the actual circumstance, for example, worrying intensely about going to the store for a grocery run. General anxiety disorder can also occur along with other anxiety disorders or depression.

- **Separation Anxiety Disorder:** This is usually associated with children and is characterized by excessive anxiety related to separation from parents or others who have parental roles. It can also happen to a person who worries or feels uneasy about being separated from friends or family.

- **Social Anxiety Disorder (Social Phobia):** If you have ever found yourself anxious or scared to interact with people (regardless of their number), or if you avoid opportunities to socialize with people, then you may suffer from this disorder. It typically involves high levels of anxiety, fear, and avoidance of social situations due to feelings of embarrassment, self-consciousness, and concern about being judged or viewed negatively by others.

- **Agoraphobia (ag-uh-ruh-FOE-be-uh):** This is a type of anxiety disorder in which a person is afraid of and often avoids unfamiliar situations or places that may make you panic and make you feel trapped or helpless. This includes very open places, crowded places, or places where it may be difficult to escape. In extreme cases, a person becomes anxious just by leaving their home.

By understanding the condition or disorder you may suffer from, you are one step closer to knowing what can trigger it. For example, if you can relate to agoraphobia, you will realize what situations make you feel the way you do.

If you find yourself knowing the places or situations that trigger your anxiety, you can learn to avoid them. However, sometimes knowing your disorder does not always translate to knowing what triggers it. While agoraphobia helps in knowing to avoid places and situations that trigger your anxiety, sometimes it can be difficult to identify the triggers in generalized anxiety disorder or panic attacks.

Bryson had his first anxiety attack at work. It was in the middle of an autumn afternoon in 2016. He had always known he had generalized anxiety, but it had never caused any symptoms until that day. He was stressed about work in general and had not eaten until late in the day. After returning from his late lunch, Bryson felt a sharp pain in his chest, and down his left arm. He began panicking and googled with conviction and fear that he was having a heart attack. He tried to calm himself by drinking some water and sitting down to relax before deciding to walk around his Vancouver office. During his walk, the pain did not go away, and it was accompanied by a strong debilitating fear that he would keel over and die alone. After managing to summon up the strength to call the emergency services, Bryson was rushed to the hospital in an ambulance. The medical staff ran some tests on him, and though he had an elevated heart rate, they found it to be within normal range. After being monitored for a few hours, Bryson was discharged and decided to visit his therapist. His therapist asked him to describe his daily routine and, after noticing a pattern, encouraged him to stop smoking too much marijuana. That, (plus more therapy and yoga), made Bryson feel much less anxious over time.

While Bryson knew he had generalized anxiety, he did not realize how smoking marijuana as much as he did triggered his anxiety and led to a panic attack.

Like Bryson, you may also be living with a type of anxiety disorder you are aware of. However, because you are so used to this condition, you simply continue managing it as it happens. But as well as knowing the techniques to manage your anxiety, it is important to also know how to identify its triggers.

In fact, one or more of your triggers may surprise you. However, once you realize them, you will be able to avoid or downgrade them and curb the anxiety before a panic attack happens. This will help calm you and free you from your anxiety shackles. Some of the common triggers you may not be aware of are listed below (Ehrenfeld, 2019):

Health: This is typically from a childhood where you may have grown up with a parent who overreacted when you (or a family member) became ill. This may have planted the seed of fear and anxiety when you or someone in your family becomes sick. You now find yourself steering clear of hospitals, doctors, and tests.

Some people who have health anxiety get scared whenever they see a symptom and some choose to ignore it because they fear it could be chronic. This is not always the best move. Other people dive into a rabbit hole of research, spending hours online trying to find more information, sometimes even while waiting for an appointment or after seeing a possible symptom. If you have been suffering unexplained symptoms, it may be best to consult your doctor and get a proper diagnosis. A doctor may also relieve your anxiety.

Prescription Medication: Your anxiety can also be triggered by prescribed medication such as birth control pills and over-the-counter cough and congestion medications. These can create sensations that become anxiety triggers for you. Talk to your doctor if you think anything you may be taking is making you feel anxious.

Recreational Drugs and Alcohol: Much like in Bryson's story, recreational drugs such as marijuana, psychedelic mushrooms and/or drugs, and alcohol may also trigger your anxiety.

Caffeine: Coffee or caffeinated drinks (such as Coca-Cola) may make you more alert and help keep you awake, but if you are prone to panic or social anxiety, it may trigger your anxiety without realizing it

Skipping Meals: Even if you cannot sit down to eat every meal, remember to eat healthy snacks like nuts. When your blood sugar falls, you may end up feeling agitated.

Bills, Taxes, and Income Losses: When you feel like you are not on top of your finances, you may start putting off paying taxes or bills. If you have ever unexpectedly lost a job or important client, you may become particularly nervous when you do not get a response to a work phone call or email. When this happens, it is important to remind yourself that every situation is different. Instead of constantly checking your email, it may be prudent to think about how you will handle the situation or try to be patient. You may even find something else to distract yourself with while you await the response. You can refer to the techniques in the previous chapter on this.

Parties or Social Events: As mentioned, one of the common anxiety disorders is social anxiety disorder. Many people are afraid of rooms of people, especially strangers. However, instead of staying indoors and avoiding people, you can bring a friend along to an event, or prepare yourself with conversation starters. You actually do not need to talk about yourself. Most times charming people are actually interested in others.

Conflict: Some people avoid conflict because of the results they have witnessed growing up. Perhaps you have seen how conflict led to the serious injury of a friend or family member. Small disagreements can trigger your anxiety as you become worried and scared that it will lead to violence.

Stress: If you live with an unresolved issue such as a chronically ill parent, family member or spouse, or bullying, you may need to monitor yourself closely. Overeating or unhealthy eating, alcohol and drug abuse, or staying up late are all common reactions to stress. Over time, these usually lead to increased anxiety.

Public Performances: While speaking in front of a large crowd, group, or just a handful of people, public speaking or performing is a fear for most of us. Though it is common and expected to feel nervous in front of people, the reactions to it can be debilitating for some. Even successful performers sometimes have stage fright, but it is how they react to it that is important. They do not let it debilitate or stop them. People often become afraid of their own physical reactions. Next time you find yourself in front of a crowd or group of people, try to welcome the queasy stomach feeling as a healthy sign of excitement!

Personal Associations: Our brains store significant memories that can be triggered by certain stimuli. For example, a smell, taste, or sound can become an anxiety trigger for you if it is connected to a bad memory or experience.

Changes in Routine: While most of us enjoy being comfortable in our respective lives, imminent change can trigger anxiety. Because we do not know what will happen when change comes, we become uneasy or extremely worried. Significant changes in your routine, for example, starting a new job, having a baby, or beginning college, can generate substantial stress and anxiety.

TECHNIQUES TO HELP YOU KNOW YOUR TRIGGERS

1. Keep a Journal: Get a journal and start keeping track of your feelings on paper. This will help you analyze what situations or stimuli trigger your anxiety. When you look back to your journal entries you will be able to establish a pattern that will show you which situation or stimulant triggered your anxiety. When you realize that caffeine triggers your anxiety, for example, you will know to reduce your intake or avoid those four cups of coffee you usually drink.

2. Look for Major Stressors: While we all experience hardships in life, the uncertainty and change in our lives can trigger anxiety. Life stressors such as relationship issues, job change or loss, pregnancy, or death of a loved one can all result in anxiety. Take a moment after your symptoms have diminished and think about what change or major event has occurred in your life. Because some major stresses are difficult to deal with on your own, it may be wise to speak to someone about them. This can be a therapist, family member, or friend.

3. Reflect on Past Experiences: Previous trauma can trigger anxiety. As mentioned, your anxiety could be triggered by a smell or a situation that you encounter. While you may not identify the trigger immediately, you will exhibit the symptoms. This means you will have an idea of what it might be that has triggered your anxiety. Take some time to consider which past negative experiences might have triggered how you feel. Think about all the things you have encountered that may have affected you.

For example, Miguel's brother was murdered at the park when he was eight. He witnessed it all and he particularly remembers how the blood stained his brother's white shirt until it was almost completely red. After that traumatizing experience, Miguel would get triggered every time he saw a red and white shirt. If you have a past trauma, certain aspects of it may remain lodged in your brain, and when you encounter a similar thing, your anxiety can be triggered. While you may know what has triggered it, you may also need to talk to a therapist about this.

4. Talk to Someone: Consult with a trusted friend or family member, because they may be able to provide valuable insight on situations that trigger your anxiety. This can work mostly if you are triggered by conflict. Perhaps you may not even realize it, but when it happens, your friends or a family member might be able to notice this and let you know when you ask.

5. Listen to Your Body: This is perhaps the best way to learn when something is off. Much like the way your body will tell you when you are sick, scared, excited or nervous, it will also tell you when your anxiety has been triggered. When your body reacts to certain stimuli, take note of what it may be. It could be something you are eating. As mentioned, caffeine, recreational and prescription drugs, and alcohol can all raise cortisol levels in your body, which can in turn trigger your anxiety.

9

GO ON A DIGITAL DETOX

> *When it comes to social media, there are just times I turn off the world, you know. There are just sometimes you have to give yourself space to be quiet, which means you've got to set those phones down.*

> — MICHELLE OBAMA

Today's world is full of wonderful gadgetry and technologies that have been designed to make our lives easier. The use of social media and professional software has enabled humans to advance in medicine, evolve in social interactions, fast-track industrialization, and improve the overall human experience. Social media platforms, such as YouTube and

TikTok, have allowed people to learn skills and tips, from how to quickly defrost the chicken you forgot to take out for dinner to tutorials on how to fix your laptop. Technology has significantly improved our lives for the better.

Unfortunately, like fire, technology, and social media can be good servants and bad masters. The prevalence of technology and social media has led to many depression cases and resultant suicides. While being connected and immersed in the digital world has become a part of our everyday lives, it has meant that we have become dependent and tethered to our devices, unable to go without them for long periods of time. Research from the Nielsen Company indicates that the average adult in the United States of America spends about eleven hours interacting with their device (The Nielsen Company, 2018). For a lot more people, the numbers are higher as we use our devices to communicate, work and get news updates.

Let's try an exercise. Take a moment and think about your previous day. As best as you can, try and think of the number of times, or the amount of time you were *not* on your phone or computer. It does not have to be an accurate number; an estimation will do. Now, compare that with the amount of time you spent *on* your phone or computer. How did you fare? Now think about this fact: In a survey conducted by an organization called Common Sense Media, 50% of participants reported that they felt they were addicted to their phones. A massive 78% of the teen respondents confessed to checking their phones at least every hour (Cherry, 2019). Now, try and imagine how it would make you feel if you were to leave the house without your phone. Do you think you will be able to manage or you will be restless and do anything to go back for it?

Because our devices have become an integral part of our everyday lives, we cannot imagine spending the whole day without them. Though using your phone can help you find distractions to silence your busy mind, there is a potential risk that you can become addicted to your device. In an effort to continuously keep your mind off the things you worry about, you may find yourself incapable of detaching from your device. When this happens, it can become a toxic behavior that can affect your ability to be productive.

When your device usage becomes excessive to the point where you simply cannot imagine going a day without it, you may have a problem and need to detox. A "digital detox" means you find a period of time where you refrain from using your device(s). This could be anything from smartphones, computers, video games, social media, and television. Detoxing from digital devices is often considered the best way to focus on cultivating meaningful and real-life connections without distractions. By temporarily forgoing digital devices, you will be able to let go of any stress or anxiety that stems from constant connectivity.

While his friends focused on their future career plans or the upcoming years of college, Christopher spent most of his time fixated on his phone, playing games and scrolling through social media. From spending hours on sites such as Reddit to games like Temple Run and Clash of Clans, Christopher left very little time to study for his final examinations. What's more, the 17-year-old would check his social media account notifications almost every fifteen minutes! He would not go anywhere without his phone. Whenever he sat down, Christopher would pull out his phone and start going through his social media accounts. He would spend, on average, fourteen to sixteen hours each day on his phone. Consequently, the results were bitter. Christopher failed to graduate due to a low-grade point average (GPA). He had squandered his final high school years wasting time on virtual relationships and gaming, which had distracted him from his studies. It increased his stress and fueled his anxiety. After failing to qualify for graduation, Christopher became unemployed for three years while most of his high school friends found high-paying jobs. This pushed him deeper into depression, and he stopped communicating with his friends and family. He began confining himself to isolation, driven by feelings of shame and self-hatred. At one point, Christopher contemplated committing suicide as he faced an emotional imbalance. His addiction to social media and gaming had snatched his final high school academic year, disconnected him from friends, and stolen his chance at happiness.

Social media has been cited as the leading cause of depression and anxiety in teenagers over the past decade. For years now, social media websites—especially image-based platforms like Instagram—have been noted to have harmful effects on young people's mental health, especially teens who struggle with body image issues. Beyond that, social media has been known to lead to problems including:

- **Disruption of Sleep:** This actually affects a lot of people. Have you ever found yourself *looking for sleep* by playing a game or watching a video on YouTube? The truth is, while you may think this works because eventually, you *do* fall asleep, your device may actually have kept you up longer than you would have without it. This means your sleep duration has been reduced, and you are getting less sleep. In addition, using your device in bed at night increases the likelihood of anxiety, insomnia, and stress (as a result of inadequate rest).

- **It Affects Your Work-life Balance:** Simply put, when you spend most of your time on your device browsing social media or your laptop working, you have less time to interact and make real-life, meaningful connections with people. Even when you do take time off work to have dinner with your family, you find it difficult to put your phone away or on silent. You struggle to resist the urge to attend to every ping that goes off from your device. Using technology excessively can make you less productive even when you are using it for work. In addition, when you are at work and are being distracted by social media or text notifications, for example, it can be very difficult to reach that perfect flow of productivity.

- **Social Comparison Causes a lot of Stress:** While scrolling through your social media, you may have found yourself comparing your own life to your friends, total strangers, and/or celebrities. Based on the small, curated glimpse you see in people's Instagram or Facebook posts, it may appear as if they are leading a fuller, richer, more exciting life. You may have

even begun comparing yourself to them,
believing that your own life is boring and sad in
comparison to theirs. This behavior has been
touted to be the leading cause of depression
cases stemming from social media use. People
who have constantly compared their lives to the
curated lives of popular people on social media
have become more depressed and unsatisfied
with their own lives. In some cases, young
people have resorted to illegal and questionable
methods of attaining the luxuries they have
seen on social media. As the saying goes,
"comparison is the thief of joy".

Monica was 15 when her parents allowed her to open
an Instagram account. She began by following all her
friends, favorite celebrities, and influencers. As time
went on, Monica became more fixated with an influ-
encer that showcased designer clothes and a lavish lifestyle. Her parents were working-class citizens who
could only afford so much. At the age of 18, Monica
moved to university to begin her undergraduate year.
In the past years, she had been so invested in this influ-
encer, she wanted to emulate the globetrotting and
designer-laden lifestyle. The only problem was, she
could not afford to buy all the designer clothes she
wanted. After one night of partying with a group of

friends, Monica met a guy who offered to take her on a shopping spree in exchange for sexual interaction. With thoughts of all the designer clothes and shoes she would buy rushing through her head, Monica agreed. Sure enough, she got her shopping spree. This continued happening for a few months, and she started to gain a huge following on her social media sites. However, in order to buy more clothes and *stay relevant* on social media, Monica began sleeping with other rich men. Her studies suffered, and she dropped out of school. After a few years, she was diagnosed with HIV.

While Monica's story ended up going down a dark path, the central premise was the seed of comparison planted by her envy and desire for the lifestyle she had been following on social media. Though most people may not suffer the same fate, more will admit to feeling envious of a lifestyle they have seen on their social media. Social comparison affects everyone—from moms' groups sharing their babies' milestones to those feeling jealous and/or envious of another person's fortune.

When overusing your device starts to dictate your thoughts, condition your behaviors, and interfere with your life, it may be time to think about cutting back and detoxing. For most people, going *cold turkey* and ditching technology completely is unlikely, because it makes our lives easier. However, cutting down seems like a more realistic approach.

Before you start detoxing from your digital devices, you may want to know if you are really addicted. Most times, we may think we are addicted because we use our devices a lot during the day. But that is simply because it makes our lives more manageable, easier, and more productive. Consider the ease at which you can check your emails from the palm of your hand, or how you can get news updates without having to pick up a newspaper.

However, when using your device begins to dictate your thoughts and behaviors, interferes with your life and productivity, worsens your stress, and brings you anxiety, then perhaps it's time for you to think about scaling it back and detaching. Below are some signs to decide whether or not you need digital detox:

- You feel anxious or stressed whenever you cannot find your phone.
- Even when you are not bored, you check your phone every few minutes because you do not want to miss anything.
- After scrolling through your social media, you find yourself feeling depressed, angry, and anxious.

- When uploading a status or post, your focus is on the number of likes and comments you will get, and become upset if the count is lower than you expected.
- You stay up late playing on your phone or watching videos and end up falling asleep later than you are meant to. You are also late to work or school because you spend your mornings browsing your social media, watching videos or playing games.
- You have trouble holding a conversation with a person without checking your phone.

Detoxing from your social media connections can be a good way to start focusing on the important things in your own life without comparing yourself to others (which only increases your anxiety and stress, and steals your joy). Detaching from your devices will allow you to focus on improving your mental well-being. However, digital detoxing does not mean you completely sever the relationship you have with your phone and other tech connections. You will not be required to throw away your phone or computer! Remember these gadgets do make our lives easier, after all. Instead, the process is more about setting boundaries, limiting screen time and making sure you use your devices in a beneficial way—rather than a harmful one that will drain you mentally and emotionally.

There may be a few things you would like to keep in mind when embarking on your "digital fast":

- **Be Realistic:** Because we are so dependent on our devices for easier communication, productivity at work and for entertainment, it would not be realistic if you expect to go cold turkey and detach completely forever. Realistically, it would be prudent to start small. You may want to try by setting limits to your screen time per day. During those few hours when you are off your device, focus on the things you like and rediscover your hobbies and passions. To be completely disconnected from a device, even for a short time, can actually be liberating and refreshing. As mentioned, completely discarding all forms of digital communication might be problematic, especially if you rely on them for work or school. However, this does not mean that you cannot enjoy the benefits of a digital detox. The key is to find time to disconnect according to your schedule and your commitments. For instance, if you use your devices during the day for work, try doing a mini detox at the end of the workday. This could involve putting your phone on 'Do Not Disturb', muting notifications, or switching it off completely.

- **Let People Around You Know:** You may want to inform your friends and family that you are on a digital detox. This will avoid any unnecessary tension and misconceptions as they might think you are ignoring them. You may also want to ask for their help and support as they can encourage you to stay device-free for that period of time.
- **Distract Yourself:** Look for ways to stay distracted. Rediscover the things you enjoy doing, such as taking a walk in the park, going to the gym, playing sports, or any other hobby of your choice.

Though it may be difficult at first, practicing digital detoxing is a rewarding process that will help you become more in tune with yourself, create meaningful real-life connections, and, more importantly, eliminate the stress and anxiety that comes with digital use. Going on a digital detox might be an uncomfortable and stressful experience in the beginning, as the mere thought of being disconnected from your device is terrifying. You can expect to feel annoyed, anxious, and even bored without your phone and/or other devices for some time.

Fortunately, here are some techniques you can implement in your daily routine to make it easier.

TECHNIQUES TO HELP YOU DIGITALLY DETOX

1. Create a Detachment Schedule: If your job involves working at a computer, it will be difficult to avoid screens. This means it becomes all the more important you prioritize detaching from that screen. Not only can it be unhealthy mentally, it can also mean you have less time to exercise or be mobile enough to stay physically healthy. In addition, excessive screen time can also decrease the quality of your vision. So, schedule a few hours per day in your calendar or set the alarm on your phone that will remind you to go for a walk or exercise. And remember to leave your phone behind when you go!

Breaks can reduce stress, especially among heavy users. You can also try powering down your device at specific times as per your schedule. For example, before dinner and until the next morning. If you are an Apple or Android user, you can set your phone to "Do Not Disturb", which silences alerts, notifications, and calls.

Start small if you must. For example, you can schedule that every Sunday (while you are not at work) you do not check your emails or messages. This allows you time to not only focus on the hobbies and non-digital activities you love, but it will also give you time to spend with loved ones.

2. Set Boundaries: This technique is similar but is actually an extension of the first one. While your schedule allows you to dictate which time you will dedicate towards digital detoxing—regardless of how busy or free you are—setting boundaries means you can use your device but only for a certain period of time. For example, when you decide to get off your computer and go to the gym, you may still want to use your phone as a music player while you exercise. You are obviously still using a digital device, but you can set boundaries on what applications or services you use. So, in this case, you can switch your phone to airplane mode, which will allow you to exercise while listening to music but disconnect you from the messages, calls and social media notifications.

In addition, you can also set boundaries by demarcating the amount of time you reserve for social media use. As we have established, social media is still an integral part of our daily lives because it allows us to effectively and seamlessly communicate with loved ones. However, platforms such as Instagram and Facebook can keep you glued to your screen for hours if you do not put boundaries to your usage. Android phones have an incorporated feature known as "Digital Wellbeing'" that allows you to monitor your screen time and also set boundaries on digital use. Apple users can also set boundaries by using the 'Screen Time' feature (found in your phone's settings) and select "Schedule Downtime". This allows only phone calls (in case of emergencies) or specific apps to still run while specified apps can be set to a specific time limit.

3. Create 'No-Phone/Device Areas': When setting limits on certain apps is too challenging or does not work, you can implement this technique instead. Remove yourself from device use completely by banning phones and screens from a specific room or area (the bedroom for instance). For example, if you always use your phone to watch videos or play games on your phone before you sleep (which reduces your sleep time), you can start leaving your phone in another room.

Cathy struggled with falling asleep at night because she would spend hours playing Candy Crush Saga. *"I will go to sleep when I run out of lives,"* she would tell herself. Sometimes, a winning streak meant she would spend almost two hours playing the game. This would cut down her sleep time. What's worse, is that in the morning, her phone was the first thing she would check after she woke up. Even on days when she would wake up early for work, she would end up being late because she would be on her phone either playing Candy Crush or scrolling Instagram until she lost track of time and was late for work. Cathy realized the only way to quit this habit was to remove the problem from the room. She started leaving her phone in the living room every night before going to bed. After a few days, she started noticing she was able to fall asleep earlier and be on time for work.

Leaving your device in another room when you are detoxing or to break a habit (as in Cathy's case) will be uncomfortable at first as you will feel an urge to roll out of bed and fetch it. However, by leaving it in another room can deter you from endless scrolling or gaming that will either make you late for work or keep you up at night.

4. Downgrade Your Device: If you find yourself having difficulty putting boundaries on your screen time or sticking to your detox schedule, then a rather aggressive technique to use can be downgrading your device. While this may seem drastic it can be equally effective. Should you be having trouble staying off your phone, you can eliminate the distractions by replacing your smartphone, for example, with a simple cell phone that cannot support apps. Depending on what you *really* need (for example, for work you may need an email app), you can downgrade to a device that supports an internet connection. However, if you mostly use your device for social media and communicative purposes, then you may want to get a basic phone that can still text and call. In fact, research has indicated that calling people instead of texting can be a beneficial way of increasing meaningful connections (Cherry, 2019). When you downgrade your device you will only be able to use it for the most essential means of communicating.

There is also a **seven-day challenge** you are encouraged to take on when you cannot go 20 minutes without checking your phone or if you sleep with it next to you. This will help you eliminate the toxicity of social media use, and the hindrances in productivity, reducing the risk of stress and anxiety associated with these.

Monday: Go to your Instagram and/or Facebook. Unfollow all the people who are not your real friends. Go to your email app and unsubscribe from unwanted email lists. Then delete all the apps you do not use (or those that leave you feeling sad or unhappy after you visit them).

Tuesday: Turn off push notifications. (Push notifications are automated notifications that are sent by an application to the user when the application is not open. They also serve to notify the user that new content has been uploaded).

Wednesday: Fight the urge to check your phone first thing in the morning. To successfully do this you can refer to the third technique of creating *no-phone* areas.

Thursday: Start charging your phone outside your bedroom. Make this your default charging station and do not look at your phone an hour before bed or after you wake up in the morning.

Friday: Go out to dinner, and leave your phone at home. Yes, this will not be easy at all. But try it!

Saturday: Spend the day off social media. Find a hobby to do and enjoy! Do not even post the pictures you take while enjoying your activity. While you may want to use social media as a *storage space* to keep your pictures, use cloud storage instead. Posting will only entice you to want to know how many likes you get or respond to the comments—which defies the logic and objective of the challenge.

Sunday: Turn off your smartphone for the entire day. Or if that is frightening to even imagine, try just switching it to "Do Not Disturb" the whole day. This way, you can silence the pesky notifications and not check your phone at least until you get an emergency call.

While all these techniques and challenges are recommended, you may have one question: *"What if my job makes it impossible or really hard to digitally detox?"*

This is a question that a lot of people might relate to. If you have a job that simply requires you to use social media, computers, and/or regularly check your emails, then the idea of a digital detox can seem very unrealistic. So how can you digitally detox if you have a job that is technology-centered? Firstly, consider doing it during a vacation, or you can even start practicing on weekends. For example, the 7-day challenge encourages you to either switch off your phone completely or switch to "Do Not Disturb" on Sundays. While Sundays are suggested, it does not have to strictly be every Sunday. It can be any day you find yourself off work.

Unplugging from your device can even make your time off better as you have opportunities to do the relaxing, non-digital things you love, and rid yourself of anxiety. You can also consider limiting certain social media platforms which still allow you to be productive. Let us be honest, chances are, mostly when you are mindlessly scrolling through social media, it is seldom for work purposes. In fact, there is probably a certain app that you always go to purely out of boredom, whether it is social media or gaming.

Finally, it is definitely recommended to get input from your boss. Talk to your manager and inform them about your plan to break your habits by digitally detoxing. Ask them if they would be okay with you taking a break for a short period, and mentally reset or recharge. Chances are, you may be able to agree on other ways to reach you (should the need arise), and they could be very willing to support you in your detox.

BEFORE I CONCLUDE THIS BOOK....

If you enjoyed this book, found it helpful, or know someone whose life could be improved by reading it, please leave a kind but honest review on Amazon. **Scan this code to go directly to the Amazon review page:**

Amazon Review

I have made it my mission to write books for those who are looking to improve their positivity, increase calm, and quiet their anxiety.
If you would like to join our Facebook community, receive notifications about my new books, or send me ideas for my next book topic,
please sign up at
harleyhunterbooks.com

CONCLUSION

Everyone experiences overthinking, stress, or anxiety at some point in their lives. While overthinking is quite normal and can be a cautionary way of keeping us from harm or repeating mistakes, it can become a problem when you can no longer keep your mind quiet or make decisions.

In some instances, you may have found yourself overthinking without realizing it, and it has slowly become a habit. You have found yourself overthinking interactions with friends or family, ruminating over things you feel you should or could have done differently, and worrying about the uncertainty of life. Though we are all prone to lament over past experiences as a way to learn from our mistakes and make different choices in the future, excessively mulling over our past only brings stress and anxiety. We beat ourselves up and think of things we should have done better, even when the circumstances were unfavorable.

In this book, you have learned how to identify when you are overthinking (and how it can cause stress and anxiety) in order to begin the process of eliminating your negative, debilitating thoughts and/or making quicker decisions.

One of the common characteristics of negative thoughts is the kind of language you use when you ruminate. As discussed, when you think back on the mistakes you have made or the regrettable choices, you often do so and use *unloving* language when you ought to be reflecting and learning. In practicing changing the way you talk to yourself; you can learn how to become kinder to yourself. After all, we all make mistakes, and how else are we going to improve and become better versions of ourselves if we do not stumble? By learning to accept our flaws and mistakes, we learn how to positively reframe our thinking and self-talk.

Positive thinking and reframing can also be improved by learning to become self-aware. When you are self-aware, you know when something is not good for you. You will also be able to understand your strengths and weaknesses and how these can help you redirect your mind from negative thoughts. Chances are you are beating yourself up over something you had no control over or worrying about something you can probably change by capitalizing on your opportunities. In addition, learning to distract yourself can also help you keep your mind off of things that would normally keep you in a loop of negative thoughts.

Through cognitive defusion, you can create space between your thoughts and yourself. By practicing exercises like "Passengers on the Bus", or "Hand in Face", you can metaphorically see how your thoughts can debilitate you and stop you from enjoying your life. We all have had times when we think our inner voices (the little red guy versus the little white guy) are trying to tell us what is best when faced with a decision. But when you practice cognitive defusion, you can weed out the thoughts that—like nagging passengers on a bus —distract you from taking control of your life and driving yourself to happiness and contentment.

Another way overthinking and anxiety can cripple you is when you continuously worry about the things you do not have and want. When this happens, it is best to pause and think about the things you *do* have. When you start practicing gratitude, you can learn to appreciate the little things that can bring you joy and satisfaction. While there is nothing wrong with wanting to achieve and attain more, becoming content with your life can give you the peace of mind to relieve the stress and anxiety associated with trying to achieve more than you need.

Learn also to limit or eliminate your choices. You can become confused, stressed, and anxious when you have too many options. These mental states can delay your decision-making, which may not always be a smart move in the business world. For example, try to keep your options limited or retain a select few in your favorite restaurant list. This helps you make easier, sound decisions while building your confidence.

In addition, it is essential to identify your triggers because while you may know when you are having a panic attack, you may be unaware of what has caused it. But when you know that drinking more than two cups of coffee can trigger your anxiety, you are in a better position to either avoid coffee altogether or limit your intake.

And although we depend on technology to help make our lives easier, it may be prudent to cut back on excessive usage. Recognize that this is not going to be easy—especially if you rely on your phone or computer for work, school, and communicating with friends and family. However, you are encouraged to utilize the techniques provided to minimize your usage and detach from the tethers of your device. As the old saying goes, too much of anything can be bad for you.

Over time, if you consistently apply the various techniques used in this book in combination, you will be able to minimize your overthinking and increase your amount of productive hours.

Consider the example of Melanie. Melanie knew her mother was prone to periods of depression, so she paid particular attention to her own mental health. She took vitamin D and B complex supplements, got plenty of exercise in the sunshine, and focused on lots of interaction with others to keep her happy and busy.

But she didn't realize overthinking could be a side effect of depression as well.

One day, she began to remodel her condo. She decided to save money by starting the demolition herself, but after a while became overwhelmed with the vast array of choices for the new layout and décor. Her overthinking spiraled out of control.

Before long, nothing was getting accomplished, the condo was in a state of half-completion, and Melanie was experiencing second guessing, negative self-talk, and choice paralysis on many levels.

Then, she applied several of the previous chapter techniques.

She would limit her choices on each item (tile, flooring, countertops, etc.) to just two or three. Her next step would be to ask four people their opinion on each item to help her make a final choice.

To further distract herself from overthinking, she took online classes in several areas (including a course to obtain an electrician license!) to learn how to install some of the renovations herself. This also aided in her ability to stop negative thinking; when she made a mistake, instead of negative self-talk, she was able to return to the online course, figure out how to correct the error, and feel positive about herself and her accomplishment.

She also maintained focus by doing a partial digital detox; she already did not have social media accounts-that part was easy! But she did like to spend a lot of time on her cell phone… so she would set goals for herself for phone and text use. For example, she would tell herself that she would not chat on the phone with a friend until she completed one targeted task.

Finally, she used cognitive defusion by accepting job assignments that involved traveling away from home; when she was not physically in the condo and focused on her job rather than the renovation, she could think back on the construction project as a whole and it didn't seem so overwhelming. She was, in essence (as explained earlier in this book), pulling her hands further away from her face and changing the view.

By learning, executing, and combining the "Stop Overthinking" book techniques, Melanie was able to focus better on the day-to-day problems at hand and move forward with the renovation in a more timely manner.

Overcoming anxiety, stress, and silencing your mind will be a work in progress. While you may have different anxiety disorders, the symptoms remain common throughout. This means you are not alone in your struggle. By picking up this book, you have planted a seed to change your mindset and quiet your mind. Using the techniques provided in this book, you can begin cultivating the benefits of the change process and enjoy the fruits of happiness, contentment, productivity, and a quiet mind.

Though this will be a challenging journey, always remember that your mind serves you, and just like a wild horse, it, too, can be calmed down—it just takes practice and commitment!

> *Keep your face to the sunshine, and you will not see a shadow.*

— HELEN KELLER

Acknowledgements

This book is dedicated to the memory of

Tony Scott

whose wonderful wit and guidance
made this book possible.

A special thanks also to

Dave Jacobs

whose editing skills kept me in check
when I was too tired to read!

REFERENCES

Betz, M. (2021, April 21). *What is self-awareness, and why is it important?* | BetterUp. BetterUp.com. https://www.betterup.com/blog/what-is-self-awareness

Barsky, A. J. & Ahern, D. K. (2004). Cognitive Behavior Therapy for Hypochondriasis. *JAMA, 291(12),* 1464. https://doi.org/10.1001/jama.291.12.1464

Bhisan, H. (2019, May 29). *What is Post Purchase Dissonance? Causes and Best Practices.* Marketing91. https://www.marketing91.com/post-purchase-dissonance/

Brewer, J. (2020, May 19). *Are You Stuck in the Anxiety-Distraction Feedback Loop?* Harvard Business Review. https://hbr.org/2020/05/are-you-stuck-in-the-anxiety-distraction-feedback-loop

Cherry, K. (2019). *The Benefits of Doing a Digital Detox.* Verywell Mind. https://www.verywellmind.com/why-and-how-to-do-a-digital-detox-4771321

Cirino, E. (2018, May 24). *10 Tips to Help You Stop Ruminating.* Healthline. https://www.healthline.com/health/how-to-stop-ruminating

Cleveland Clinic. (2022, May 17). *Overthinking Disorder: Is It a Mental Illness?* Cleveland Clinic. https://health.clevelandclinic.org/is-over thinking-a-mental-illness/

Di Schiena, R., Luminet, O., Chang, B. & Philippot, P. (2013). Why are Depressive Individuals Indecisive? Different Modes of Rumination Account for Indecision in Non-clinical Depression. *Cognitive Therapy and Research, 37(4),* 713–724. https://doi.org/10.1007/s10608-012-9517-9

Duval, S. & Wicklund, R. A. (1972). *A theory of objective self-awareness.* Academic Press.

Ehrenfeld, T. (2019, May 29). *What Triggers Your Anxiety?* | *Psychology Today.* www.psychologytoday.com. https://www.psychologytoday.com/us/blog/open-gently/201905/what-triggers-your-anxiety

Eurich, T. (2018, January 4). *What Self-Awareness Really Is (and How to Cultivate It)*. Harvard Business Review. https://hbr.org/2018/01/what-self-awareness-really-is-and-how-to-cultivate-it

Fader, S. (2021, February 22). *What Is Overthinking Disorder? | BetterHelp*. www.betterhelp.com. https://www.betterhelp.com/advice/personality-disorders/what-is-overthinking-disorder/

Hall, C. B. & Lundh, L. G. (2018). Brief Therapist-Guided Exposure Treatment of Panic Attacks: A Pilot Study. *Behavior Modification, 43(4)*, 564–586. https://doi.org/10.1177/0145445518776472

Hull, M. (2021, May 26). *Identifying & Coping with Anxiety Triggers | The Recovery Village*. The Recovery Village Drug and Alcohol Rehab. https://www.therecoveryvillage.com/mental-health/anxiety/anxiety-triggers/

Hasan, S. (2019, July 12). *How Overthinking Can Affect Mental and Physical Health*. KERA News. https://www.keranews.org/health-science-tech/2019-07-12/how-overthinking-can-affect-mental-and-physical-health

Holas, P., Krejtz, I., Rusanowska, M., Rohnka, N. & Nezlek, J. B. (2018). Attention to negative words predicts daily rumination among people with clinical depression: evidence from an eye tracking and daily diary study. *Cognition and Emotion, 33(6)*, 1277–1283. https://doi.org/10.1080/02699931.2018.1541168

Juma, N. (Ed.). (2022, May 4). Quotes to Help You Build a Growth Mindset. Everyday Power. https://everydaypower.com/mindset-quotes/

Kinderman, P., Schwannauer, M., Pontin, E. & Tai, S. (2013). Psychological Processes Mediate the Impact of Familial Risk, Social Circumstances and Life Events on Mental Health. *PLoS ONE, 8(10)*, e76564. https://doi.org/10.1371/journal.pone.0076564

Krstic, Z. (2021, June 7). *8 Ways to Quit Overthinking Every Little Thing, According to Experts*. Good Housekeeping. https://www.goodhousekeeping.com/health/a36411708/how-to-stop-overthinking/

Lamothe, C. (2019, November 15). *How to Stop Overthinking: 14 Strategies*. Healthline. https://www.healthline.com/health/how-to-stop-overthinking

Lebow, H. I. (2016, May 17). *What is Emotional Intelligence (EQ)?* Psych Central. https://psychcentral.com/lib/what-is-emotional-intelligence-eq

Maenpaa, J. (2022, February 25). *A psychotherapist shares the 3 exercises she uses every day "to stop overthinking."* CNBC. https://www.cnbc.com/2022/02/25/a-psychotherapist-shares-the-exercises-she-uses-every-day-to-stop-overthinking.html

Marsh, A. (2022, May 22). *Social Anxiety Disorder (SAD).* Verywell Mind. https://www.verywellmind.com/social-anxiety-disorder-overview-4581773

Mayo Clinic. (2018a). *Anxiety disorders - symptoms and causes.* Mayo Clinic; Mayo Foundation for Medical Education and Research. https://www.mayoclinic.org/diseases-conditions/anxiety/symptoms-causes/syc-20350961

Mayo Clinic. (2018b). *Illness anxiety disorder - Symptoms and causes.* Mayo Clinic. https://www.mayoclinic.org/diseases-conditions/illness-anxiety-disorder/symptoms-causes/syc-20373782

McCallum, K. (2021, April 12). *When Overthinking Becomes a Problem & What You Can Do About It.* www.houstonmethodist.org. https://www.houstonmethodist.org/blog/articles/2021/apr/when-overthinking-becomes-a-problem-and-what-you-can-do-about-it/

Miller, J. (2016, July 6). *8 Ways To Have More Gratitude Every Day.* Forbes. https://www.forbes.com/sites/womensmedia/2016/07/08/8-ways-to-have-more-gratitude-every-day/?sh=164c12f81d54

Mishra, K. (2021, December 31). *Overthinking? Deal with it before it destroys your peace of mind.* Healthshots. https://www.healthshots.com/mind/mental-health/overthinking-and-its-impact-on-your-mental-health-know-from-an-expert/

Morin, A. (2020, April 20). *10 Signs You're Overthinking (And What To Do About It).* Forbes. https://www.forbes.com/sites/amymorin/2020/04/20/10-signs-youre-overthinking-and-what-to-do-about-it/?sh=550ec31b2bb8

Morin, A. (2020, September 27). *Are You Overthinking? Here's How to Tell.* Verywell Mind. https://www.verywellmind.com/how-to-know-when-youre-overthinking-5077069

Morin, A. (2022, March 4). *Self-Awareness and Learning Differences.*Understood.org. https://www.understood.org/en/arti cles/the-importance-of-self-awareness

Nast, C. (2018, June 1). *What's the Difference Between Occasional Obsessive Thoughts and OCD?* SELF. https://www.self.com/story/difference-between-occasional-obsessive-thoughts-ocd

Nayeem, T. & Casidy, R. (2013). The role of external influences in high involvement purchase behavior. *Marketing Intelligence & Planning, 31*(7), 732–745. https://doi.org/10.1108/mip-02-2013-0030

Newman, T. (2017, July 24). *Hypochondria: What is illness anxiety disorder?* www.medicalnewstoday.com. https://www.medicalnewstoday.com/articles/9983#symptoms

Sengar, C. (2022, May 20). *Overthinking Is Bad For Mental Health, Here Is How To Stop Doing That.* Onlymyhealth. https://www.onlymyhealth.com/overthinking-causes-effects-tips-to-avoid-1653031620

Star, K. (2020, September 17). *How to Distract Yourself From Panic Disorder.* Verywell Mind. https://www.verywellmind.com/distrac tion-techniques-for-panic-disorder-2584138

Sturt, D. & Nordstrom, T. (2015, June 11). *Decision-Paralysis: Why It's Prevalent And Three Ways To End It.* Forbes. https://www.forbes.com/sites/davidsturt/2015/06/11/decision-paralysis-why-its-prevalent-and-3-ways-to-end-it/?sh=5e7739bd35b2

The Nelson Company. (July 2018). *The Nielsen Total Audience Report: Q1 2018.* https://www.nielsen.com/us/en/insights/report/2018/q1-2018-total-audience-report/

Washington Center for Cognitive Therapy. (2014). *Cognitive Defusion.* The Washington Center for Cognitive Therapy. https://washington centerforcognitivetherapy.com/cognitive-defusion/

Wilson, T. D. & Schooler, J. W. (1991). Thinking too much: Introspection can reduce the quality of preferences and decisions. *Journal of Personality and Social Psychology, 60*(2), 181–192. https://doi.org/10.1037/0022-3514.60.2.181

Villines, Z. (2021, March 31). *Toxic positivity: Definition, risks, how to avoid, and more.* Www.medicalnewstoday.com. https://www.medicalnewstoday.com/articles/toxic-positivity